Cartoons by Tim Whyatt
All images ©Tim Whyatt 2002-2017

Published by Studio Press
An imprint of Kings Road Publishing. Part of Bonnier Publishing
The Plaza, 535 King's Road, London, SW10 0SZ

www.bonnierpublishing.co.uk

Printed in Italy   10 9 8 7 6 5 4 3 2 1

SENIOR MOMENTS

Christmas

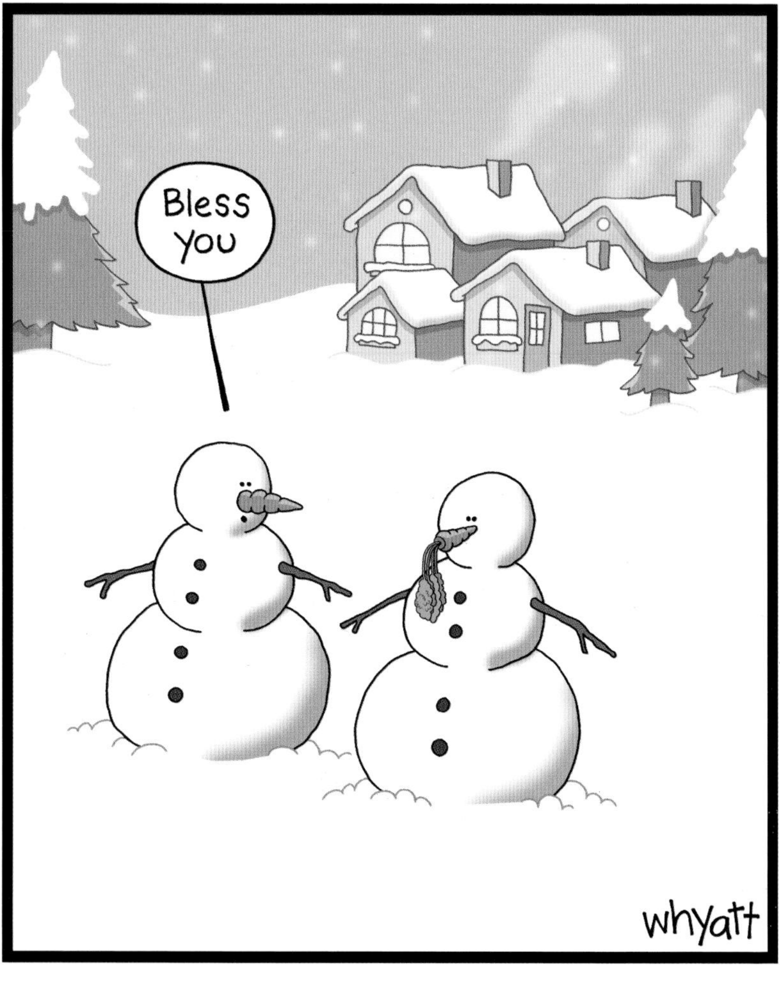
Bless you
whyatt

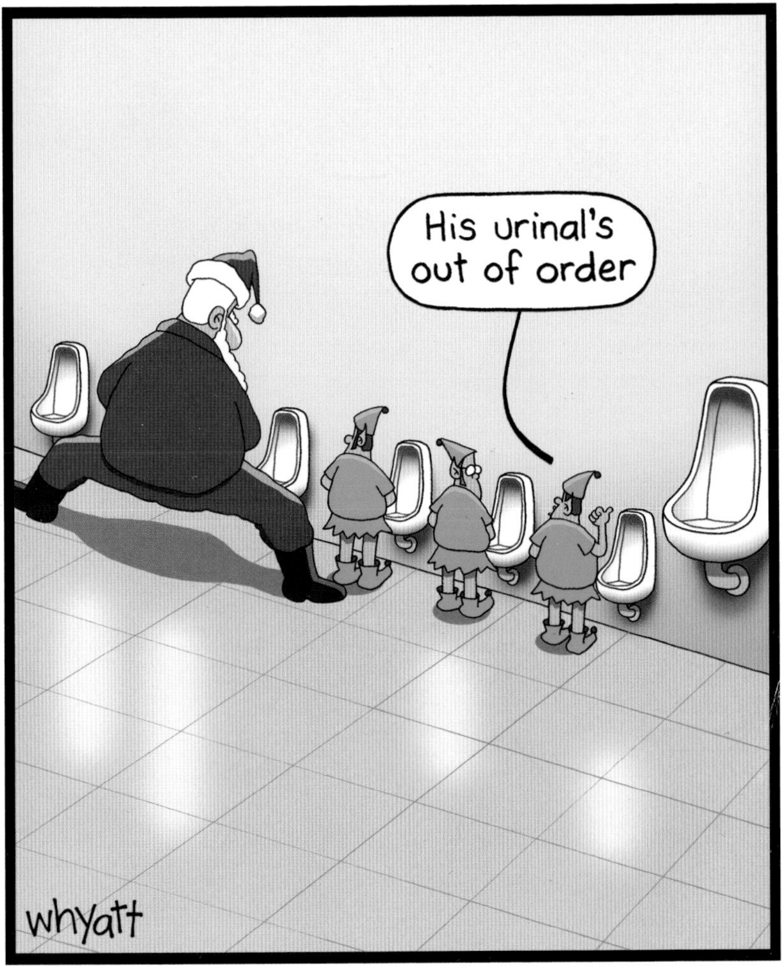
His urinal's out of order
whyatt

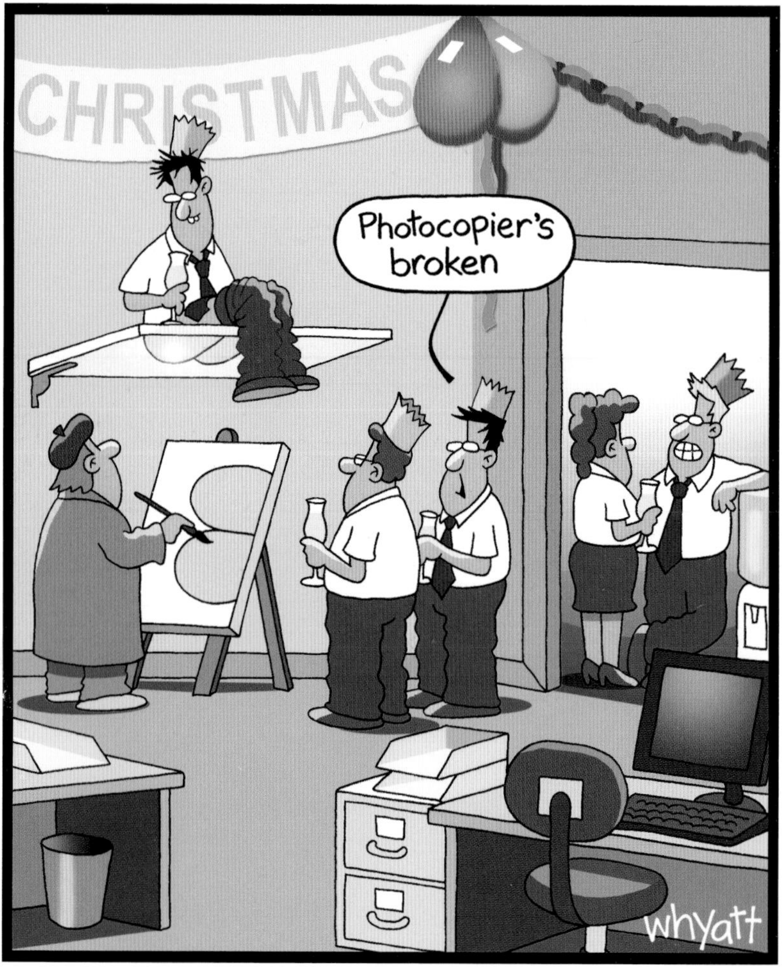
CHRISTMAS
Photocopier's broken
whyatt

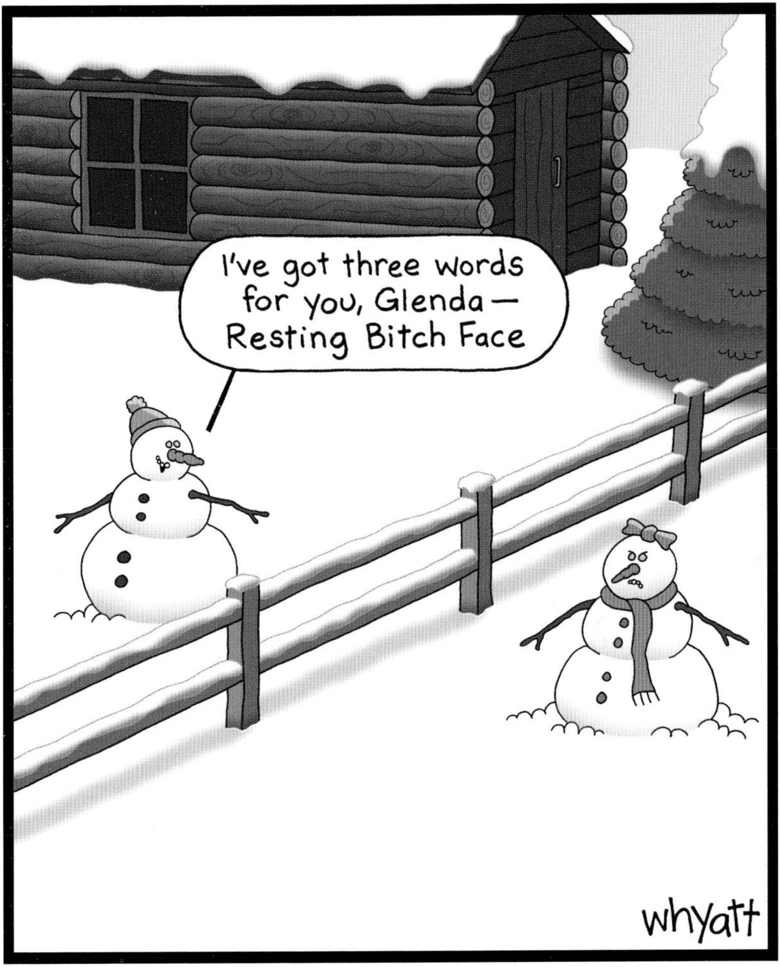
I've got three words for you, Glenda— Resting Bitch Face
whyatt

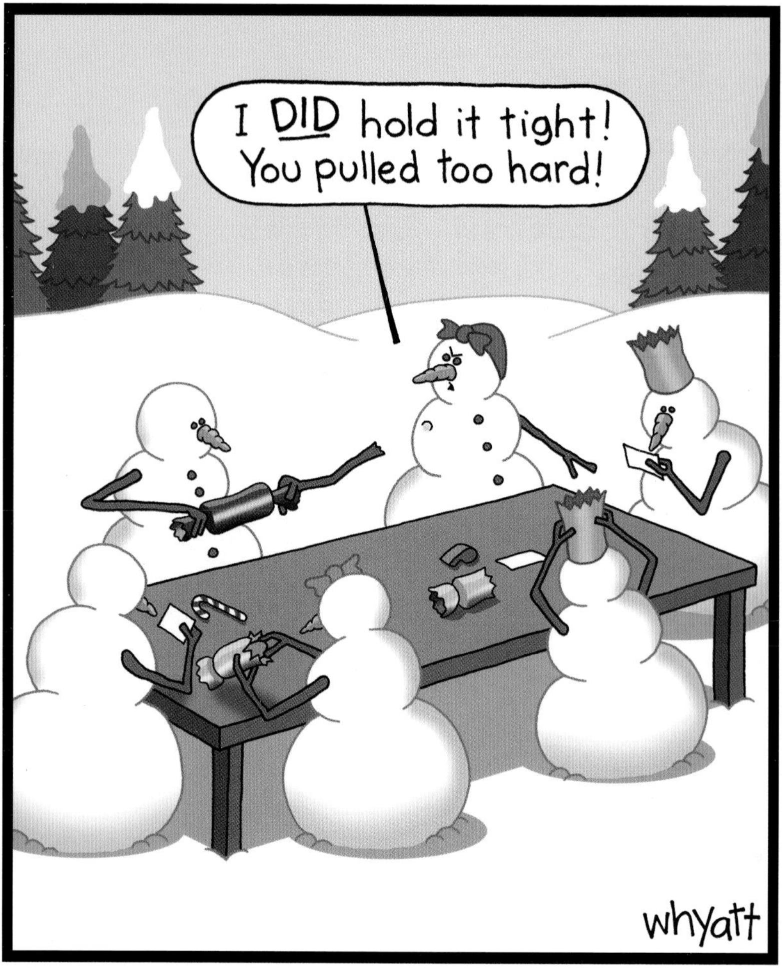
I DID hold it tight! You pulled too hard!
whyatt

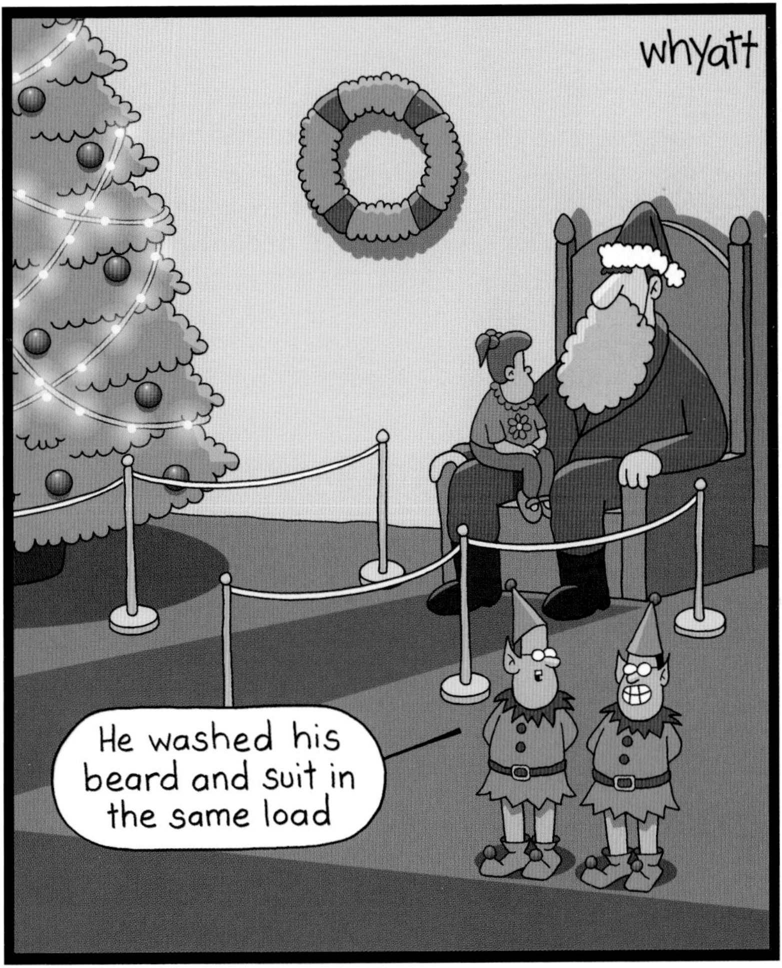
whyatt
He washed his beard and suit in the same load

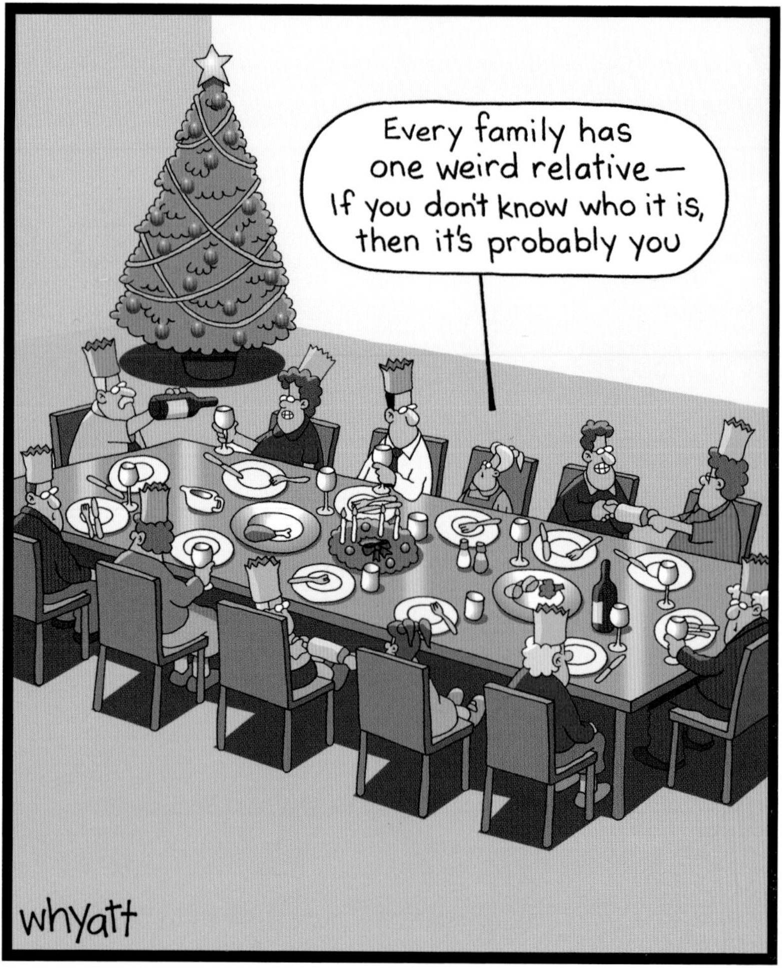
Every family has one weird relative — If you don't know who it is, then it's probably you
whyatt

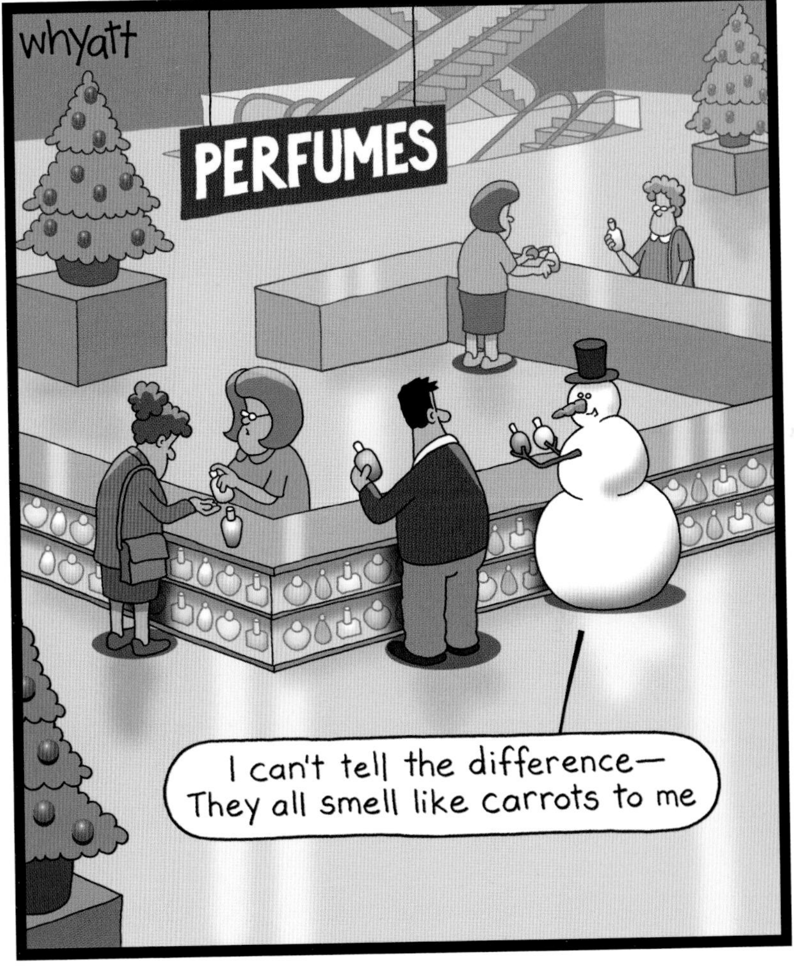
whyatt
PERFUMES
I can't tell the difference—
They all smell like carrots to me

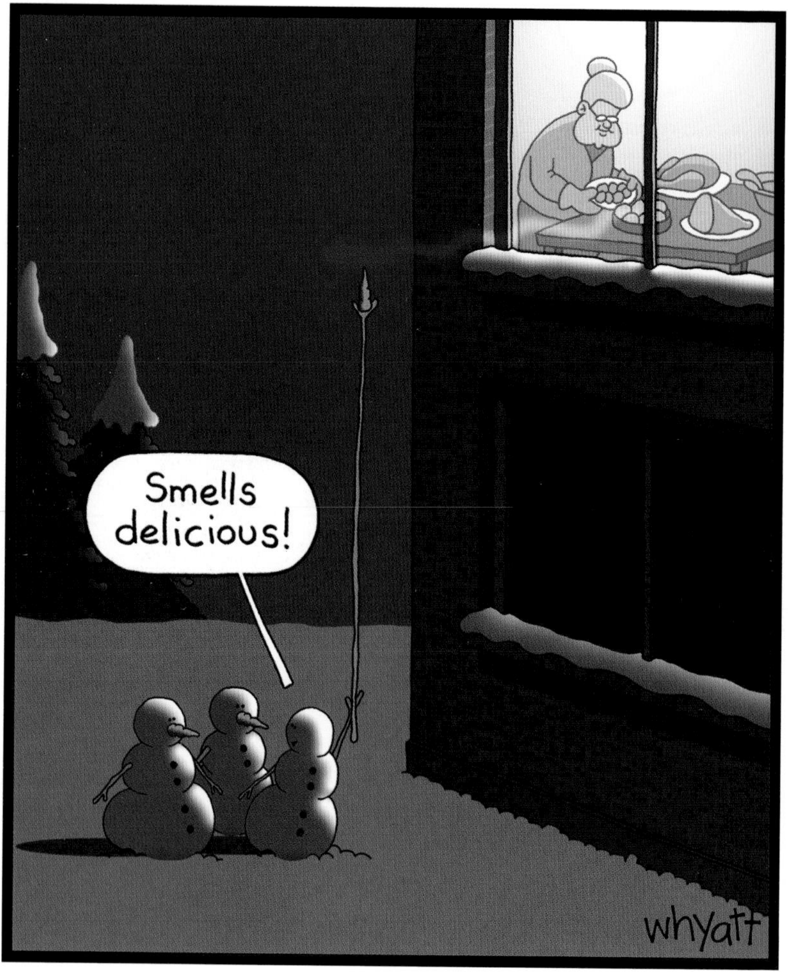
Smells delicious!
whyatt

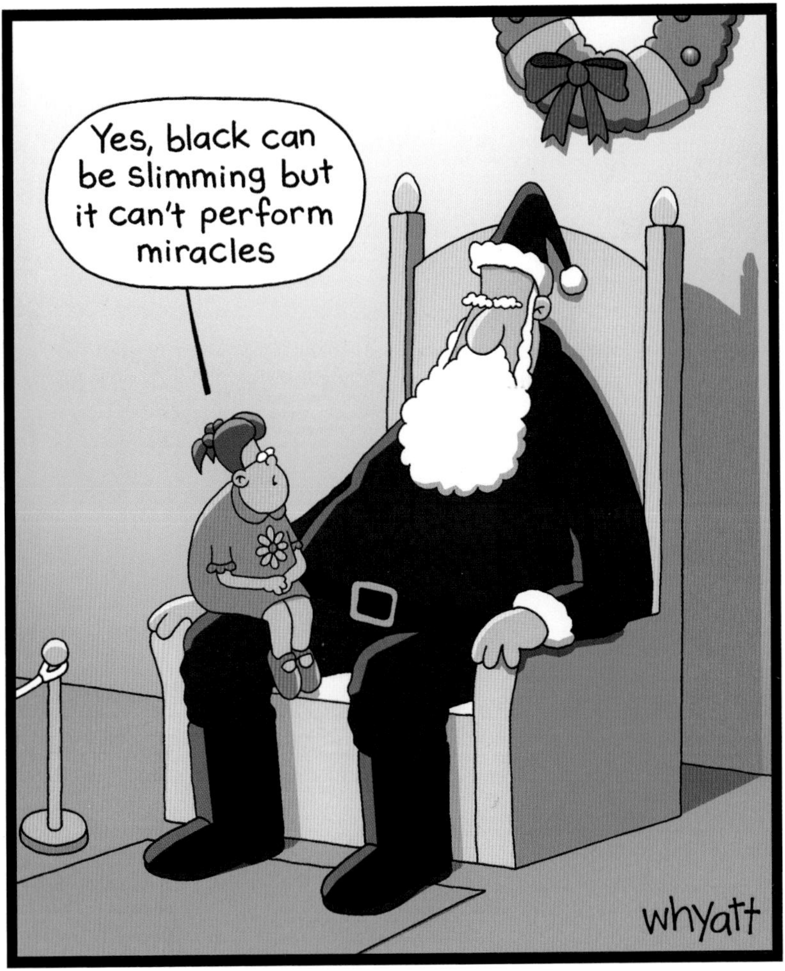
Yes, black can be slimming but it can't perform miracles
whyatt

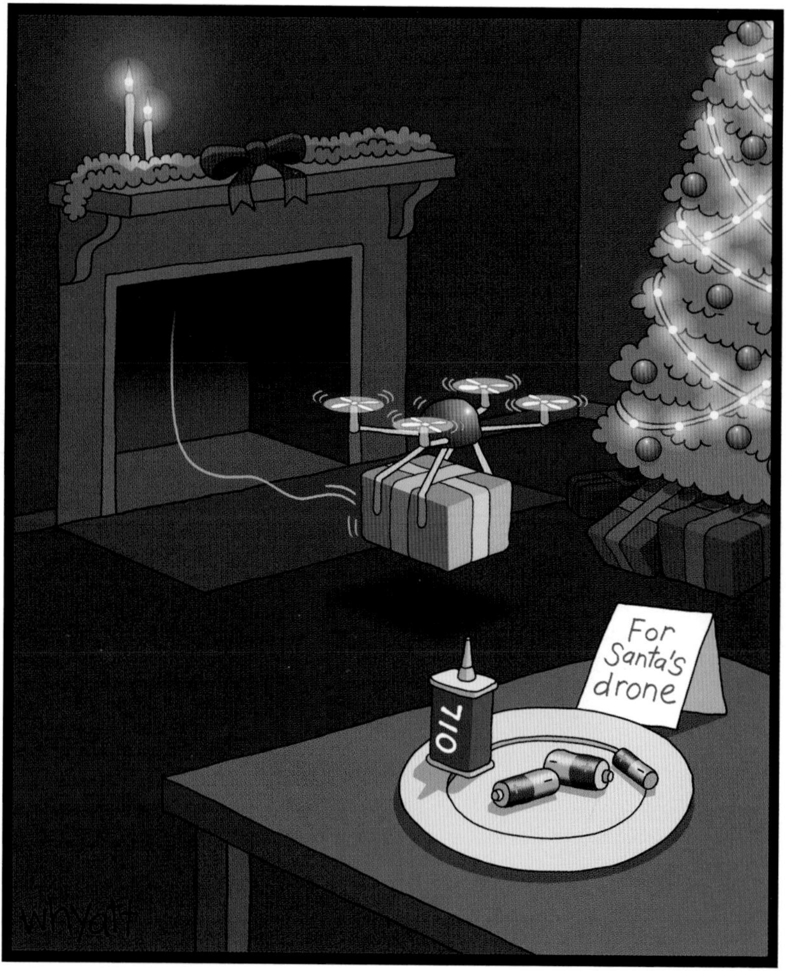
For Santa's drone
OIL

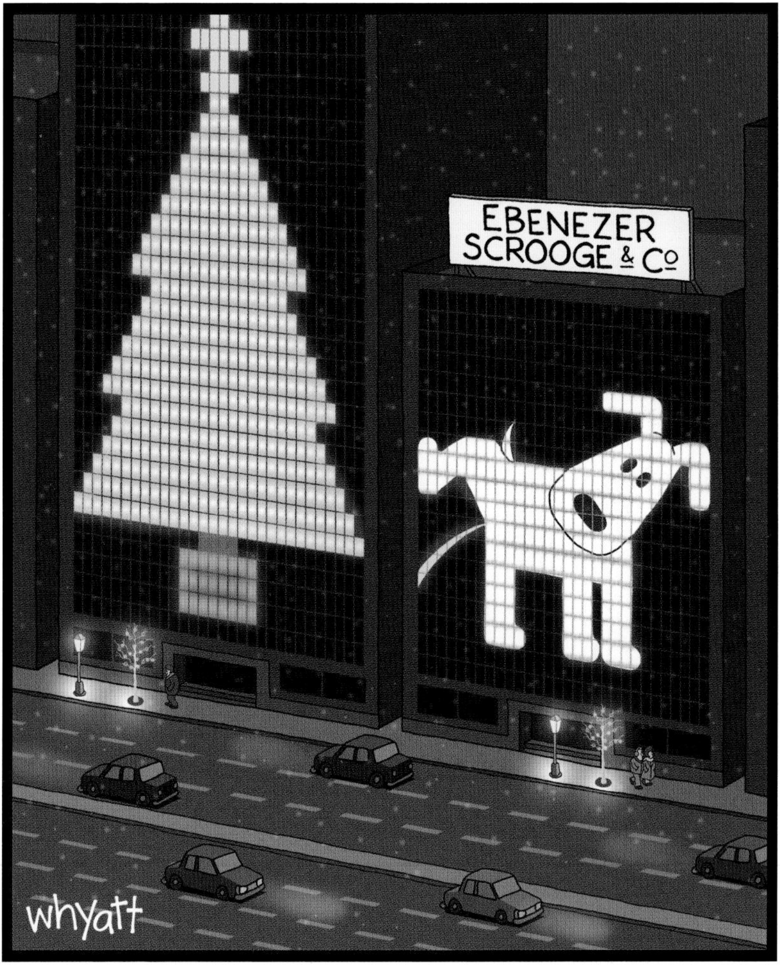
EBENEZER
SCROOGE & Co
whyatt

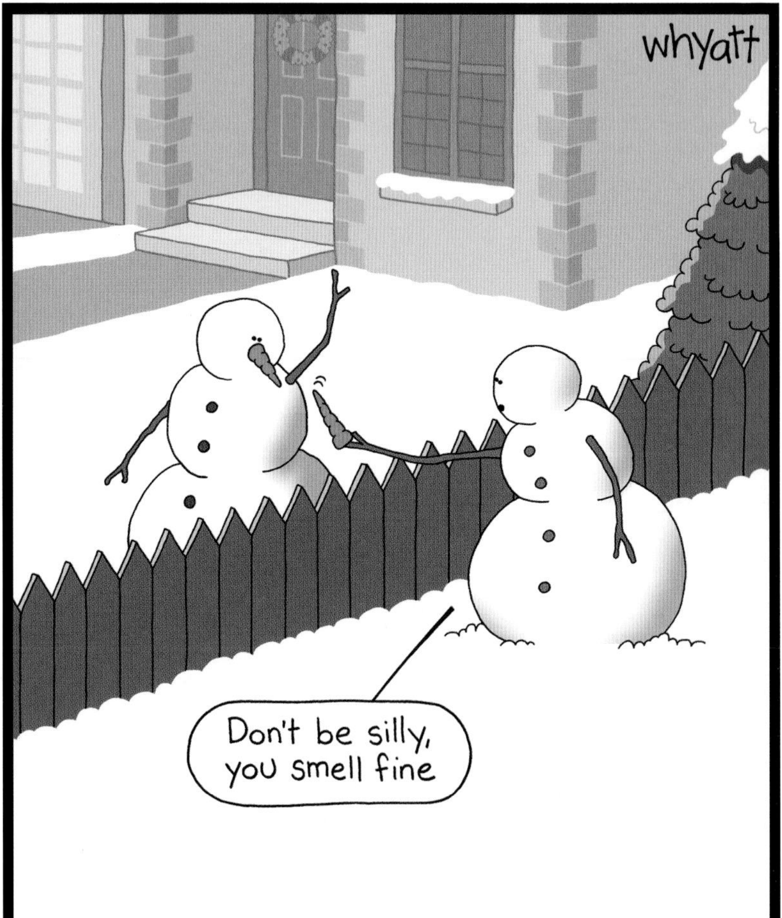
whyatt
Don't be silly, you smell fine

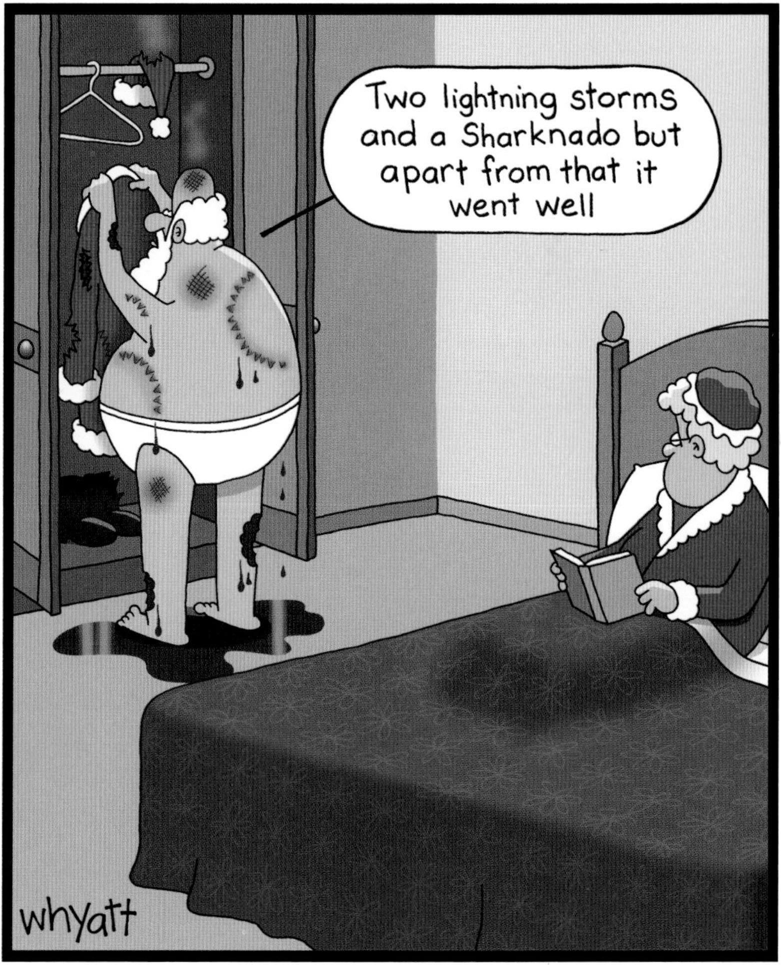
Two lightning storms and a Sharknado but apart from that it went well
whyatt

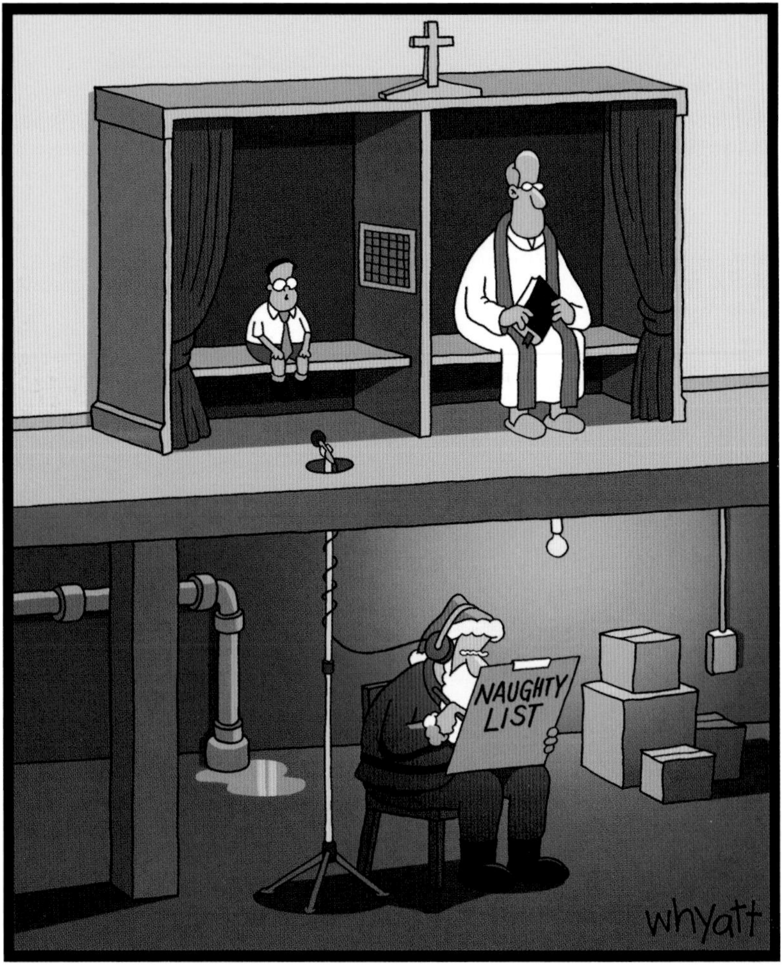
NAUGHTY LIST
whyatt

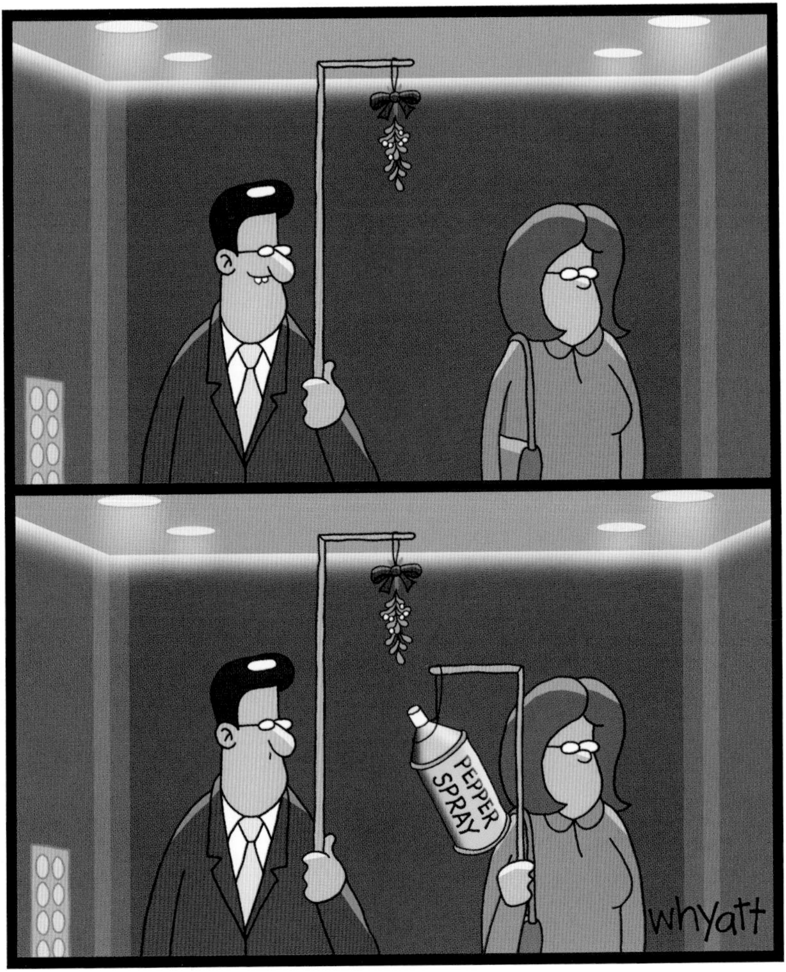
PEPPER SPRAY
whyatt

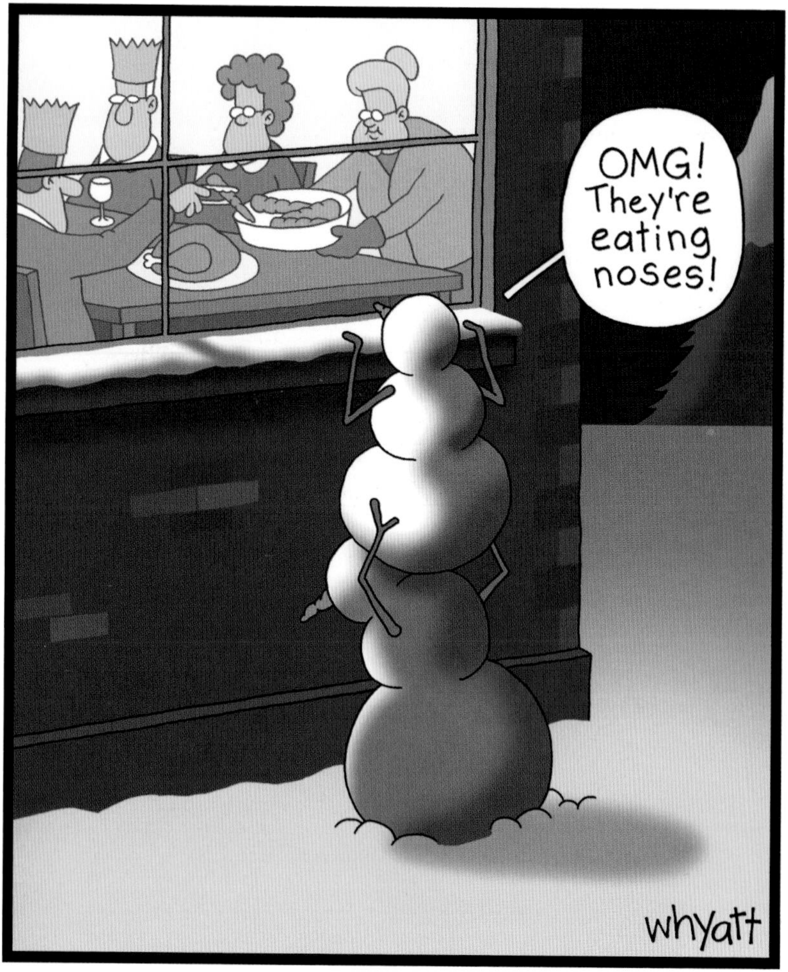
OMG! They're eating noses!
whyatt

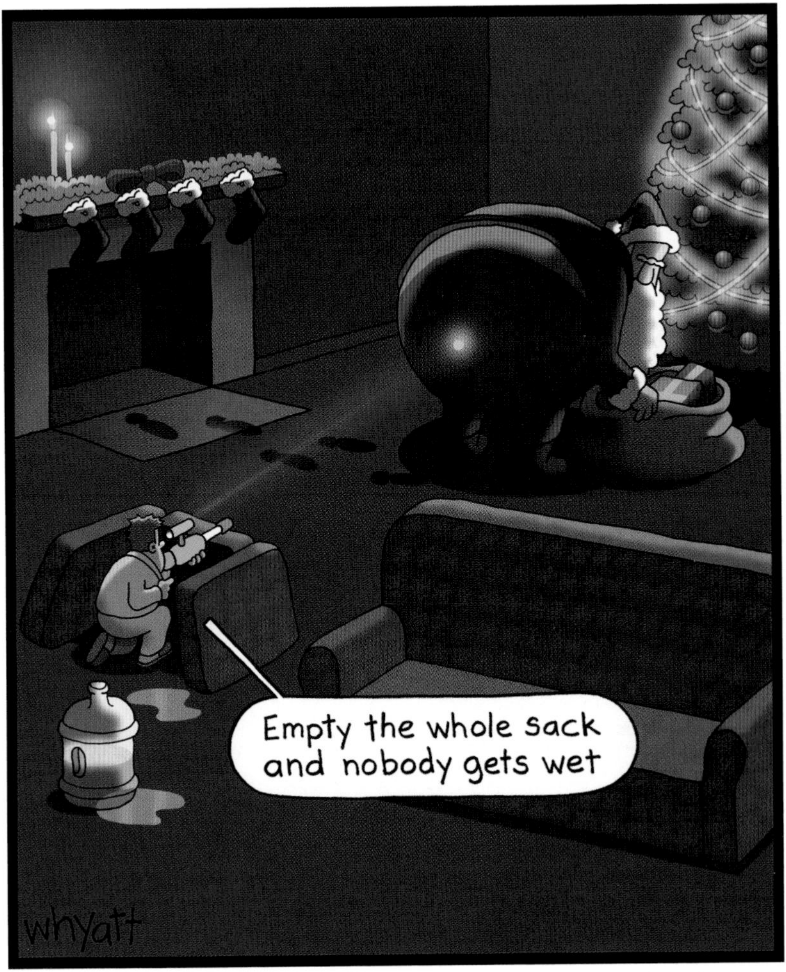
Empty the whole sack
and nobody gets wet
whyatt

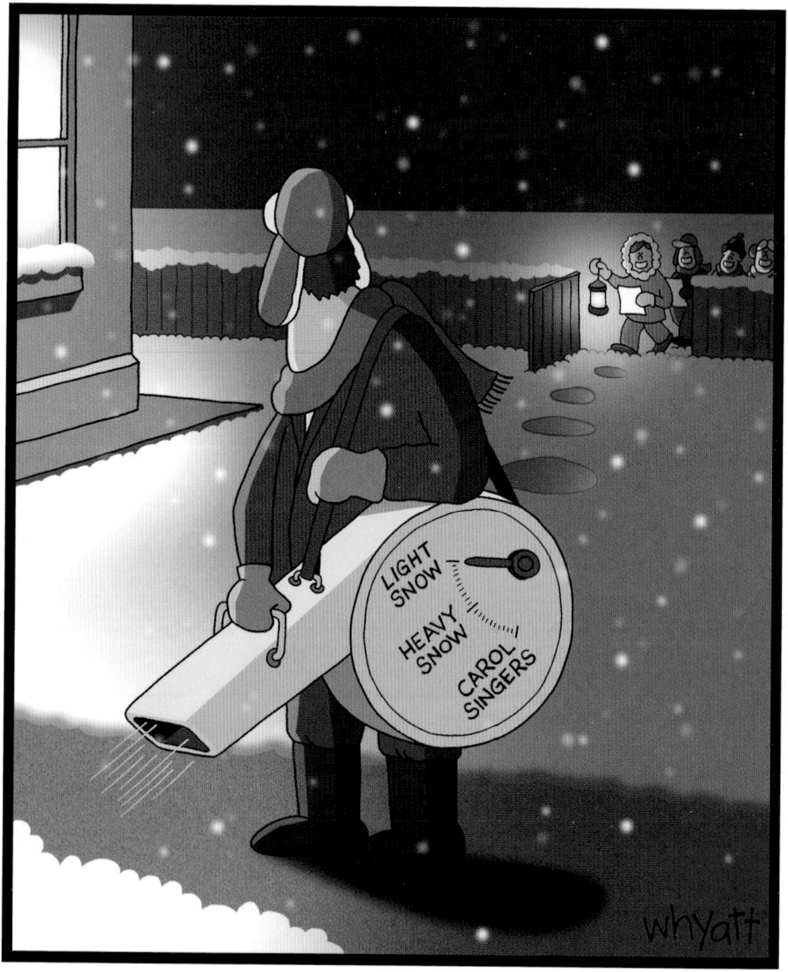
LIGHT SNOW
HEAVY SNOW
CAROL SINGERS
whyatt

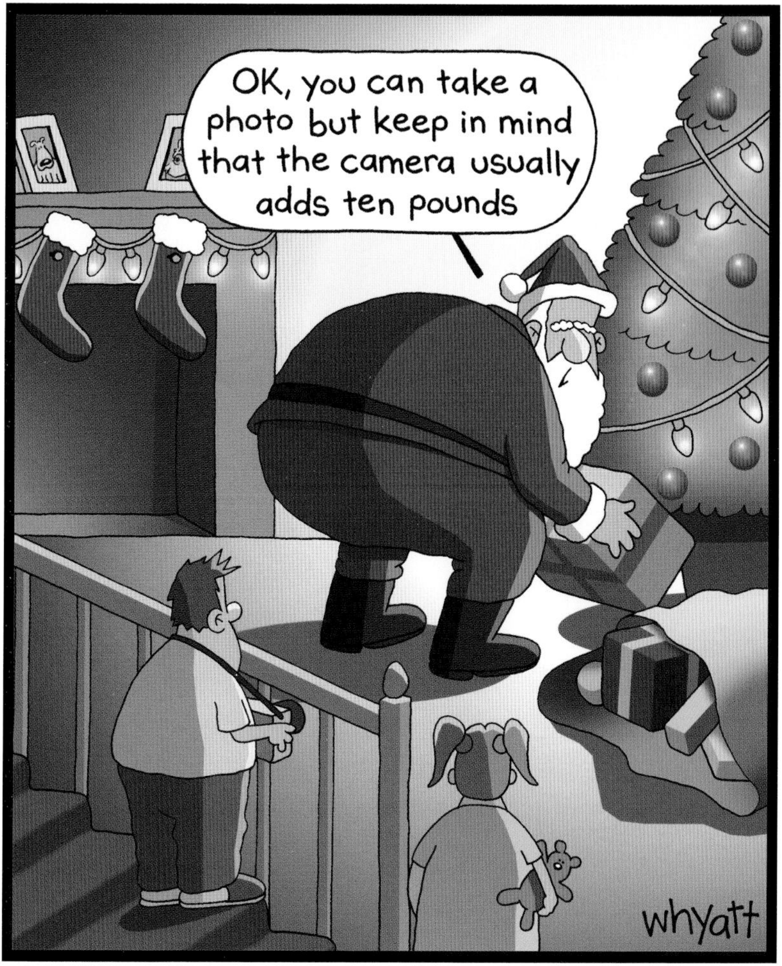
OK, you can take a photo but keep in mind that the camera usually adds ten pounds
whyatt

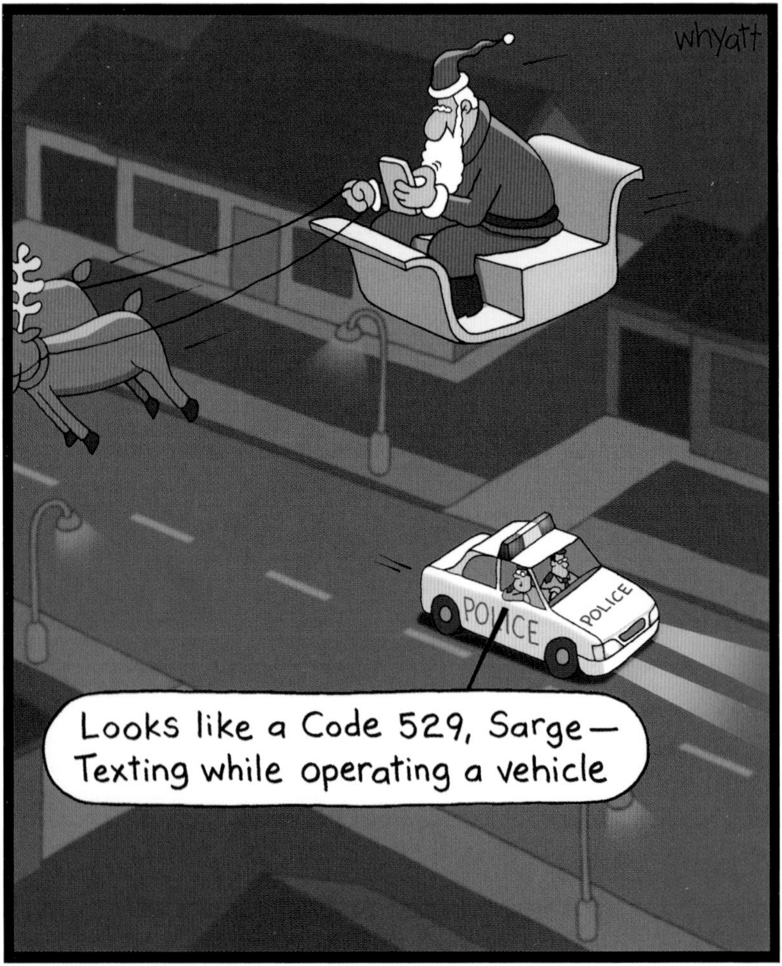
whyatt
POLICE
POLICE
Looks like a Code 529, Sarge—
Texting while operating a vehicle

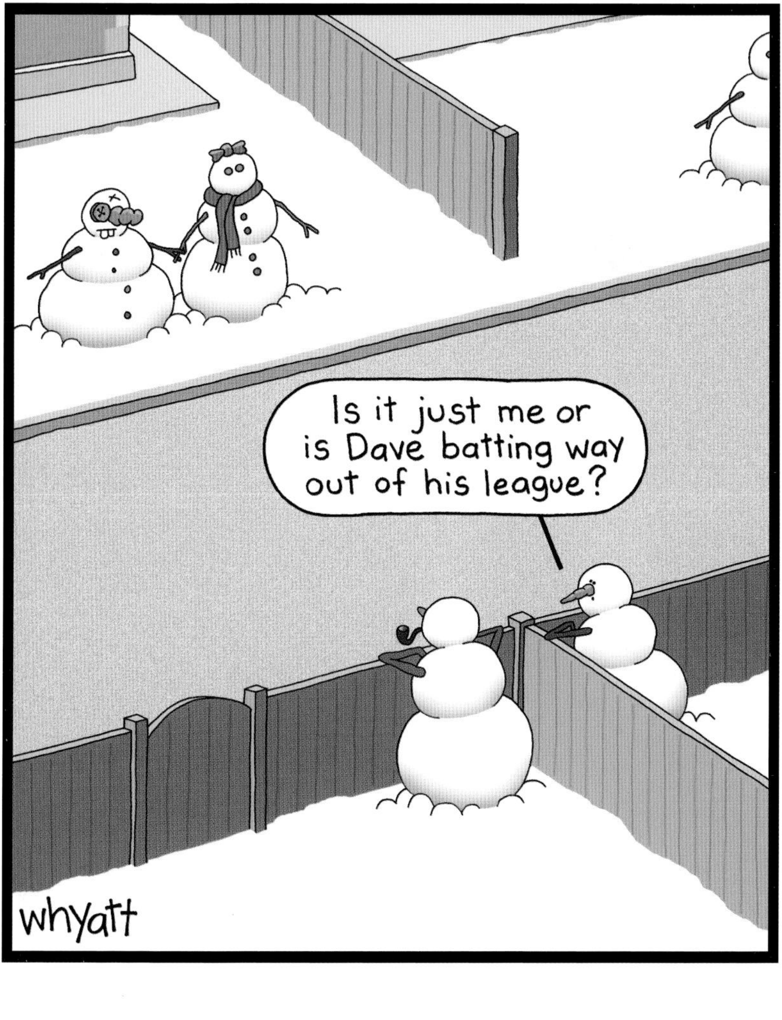
Is it just me or is Dave batting way out of his league?
whyatt

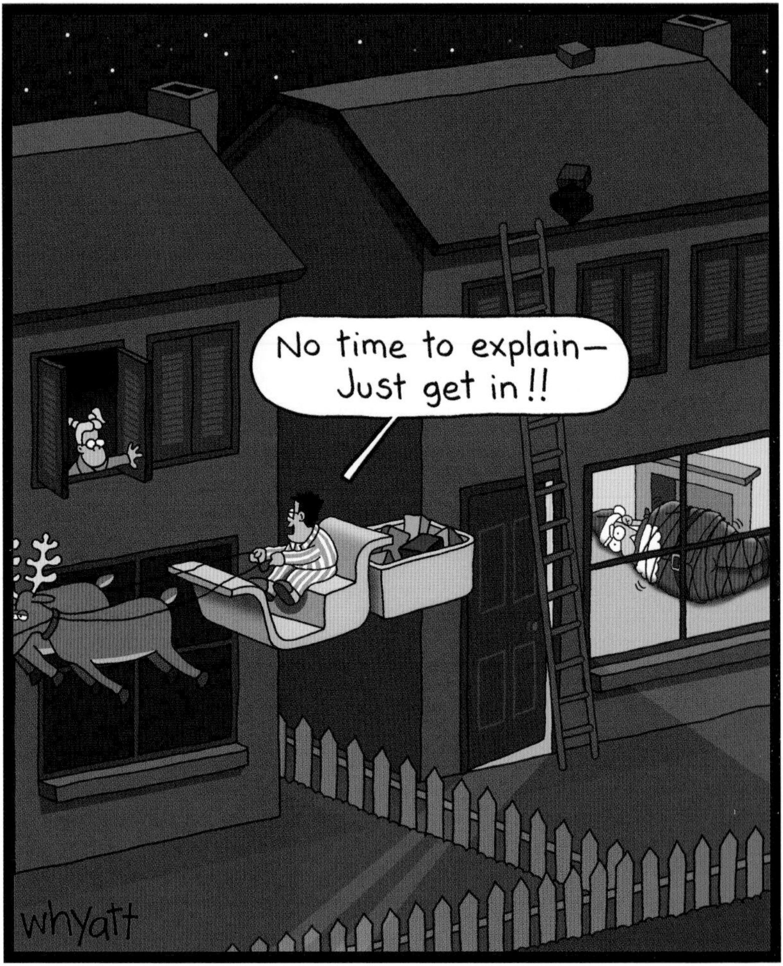
No time to explain—
Just get in!!
whyatt

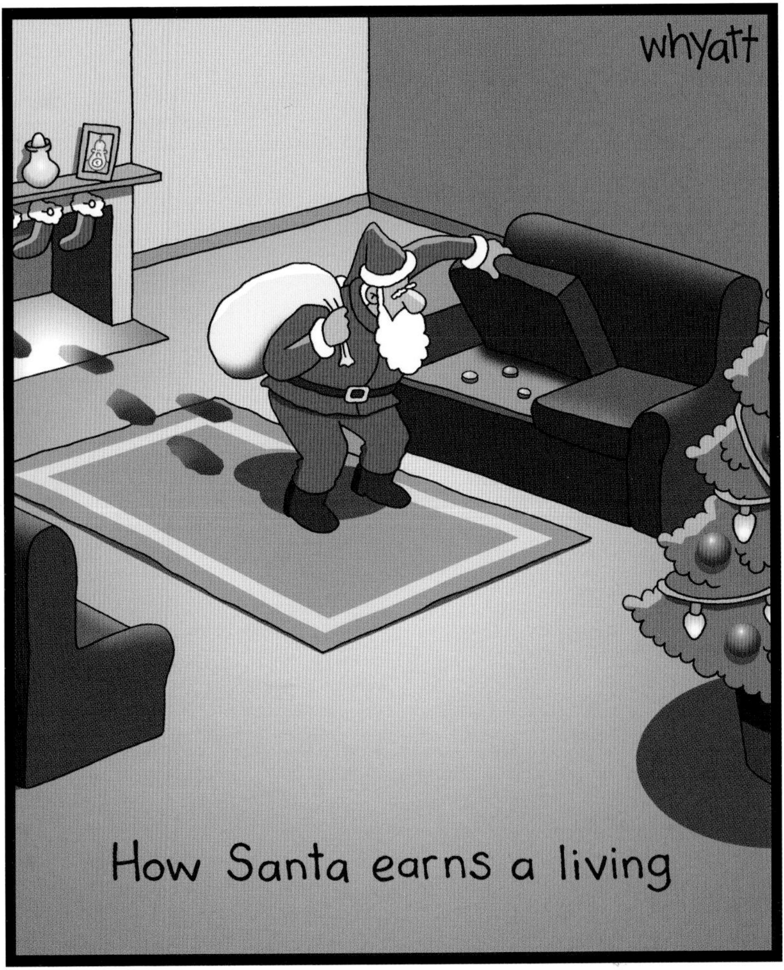
whyatt

How Santa earns a living

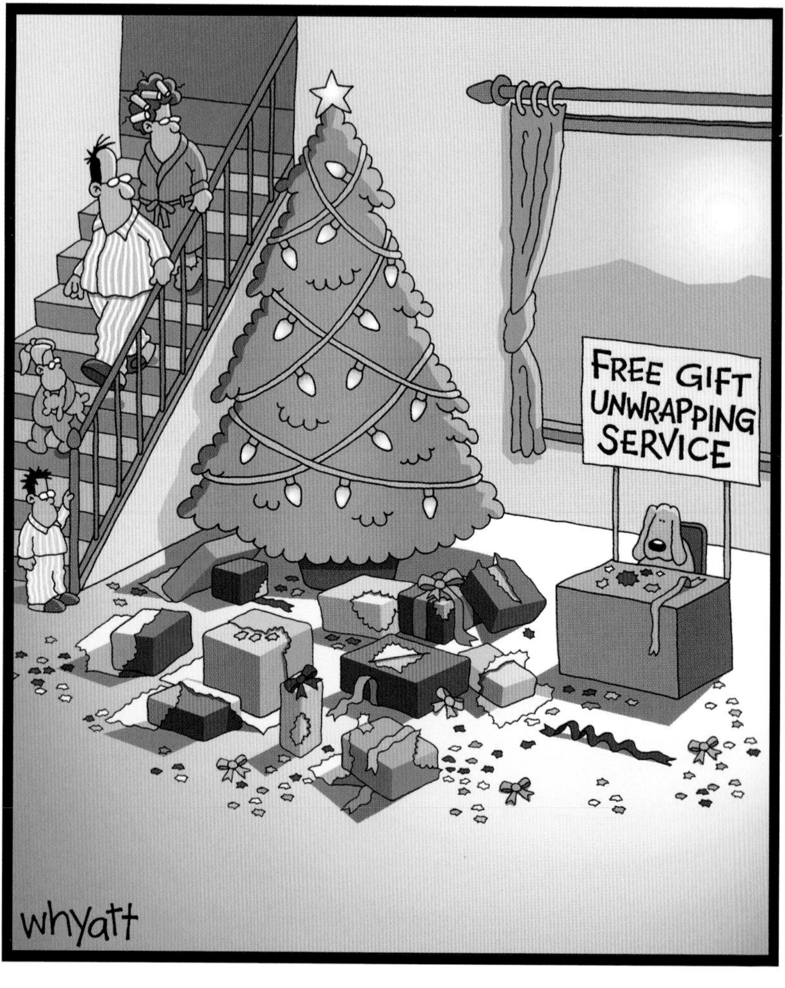
FREE GIFT UNWRAPPING SERVICE
whyatt

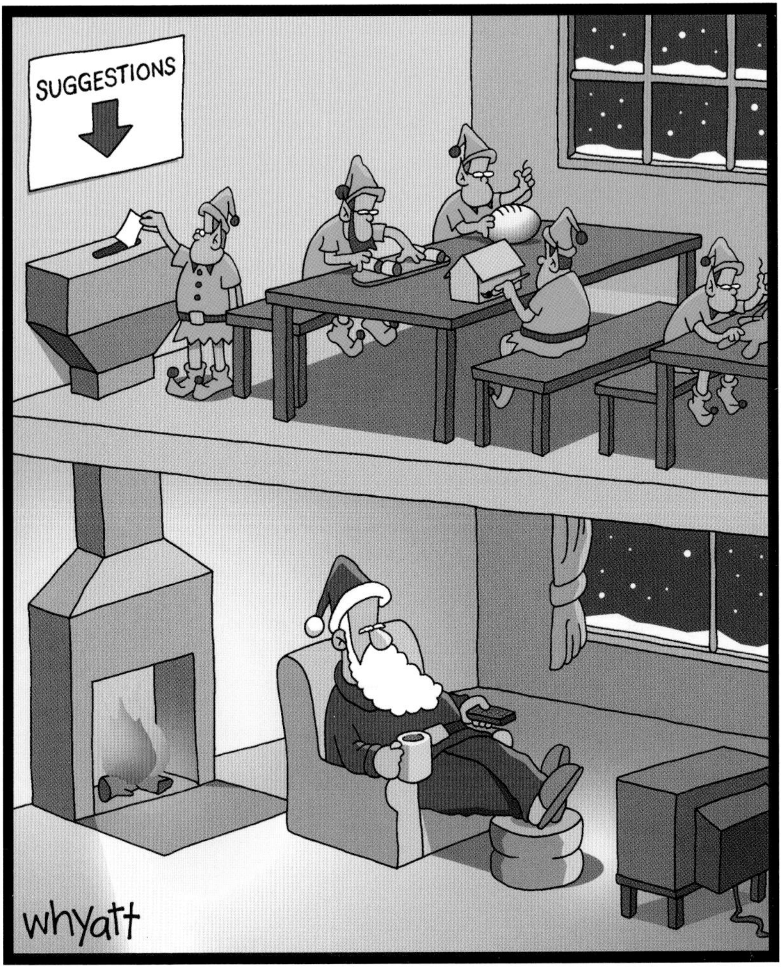
SUGGESTIONS
whyatt

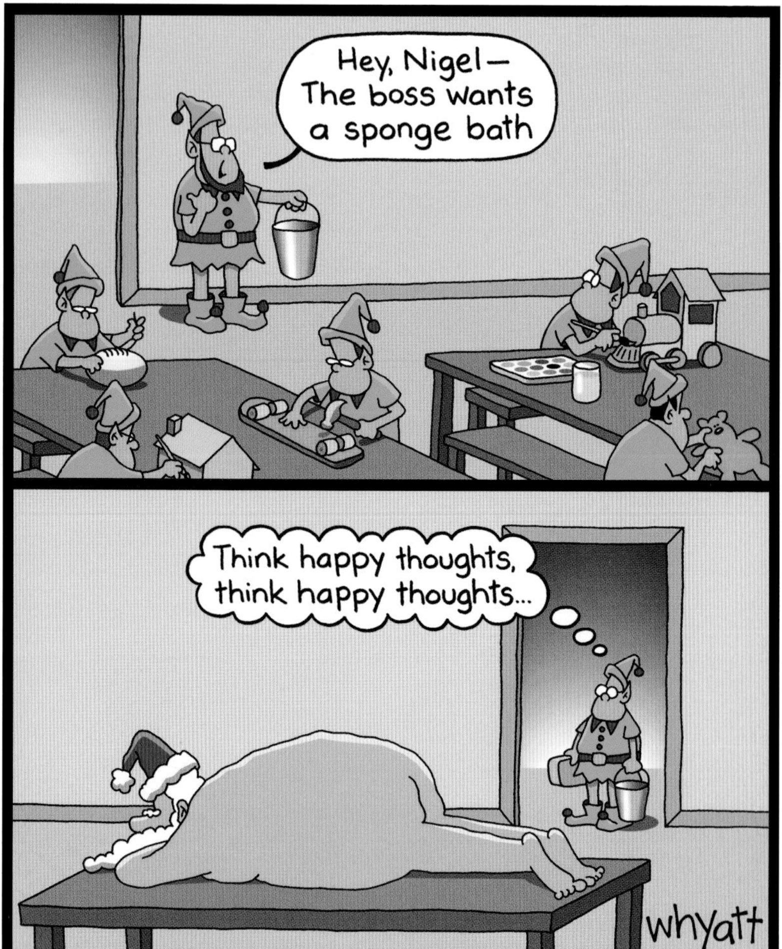
Hey, Nigel—
The boss wants
a sponge bath
Think happy thoughts,
think happy thoughts...
whyatt

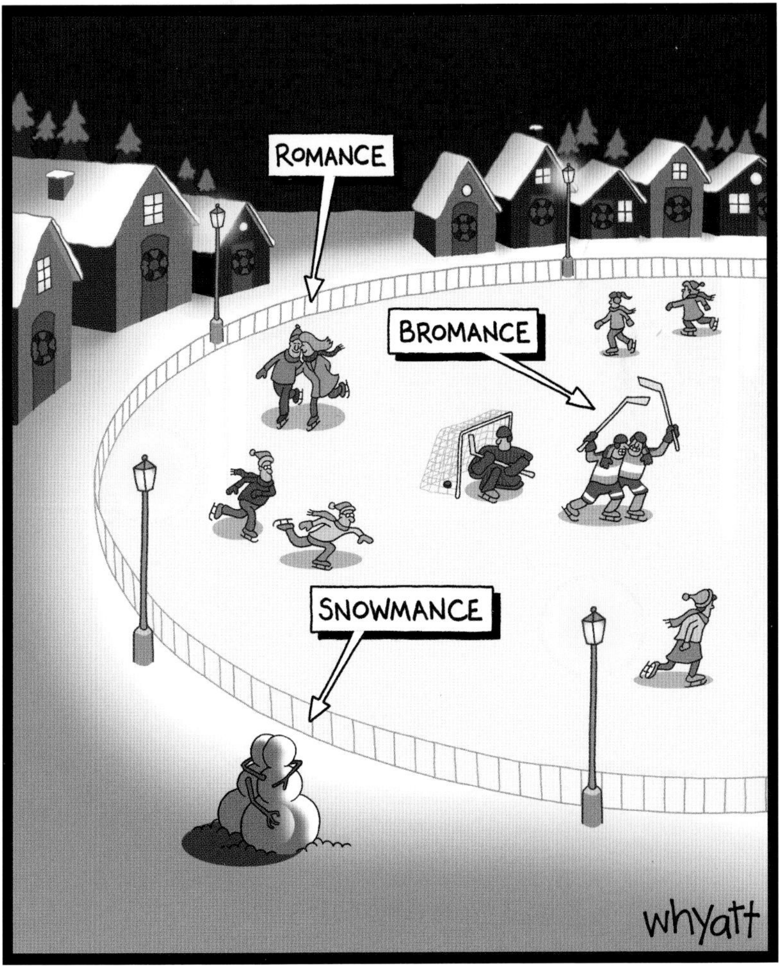
ROMANCE
BROMANCE
SNOWMANCE
whyatt

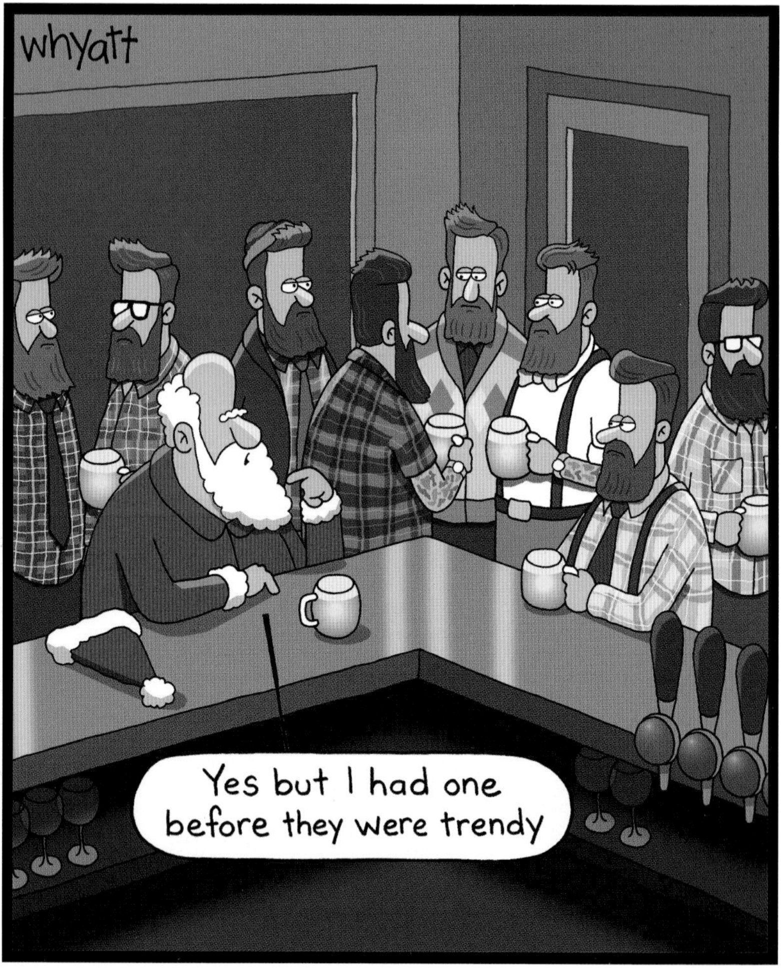
whyatt
Yes but I had one before they were trendy

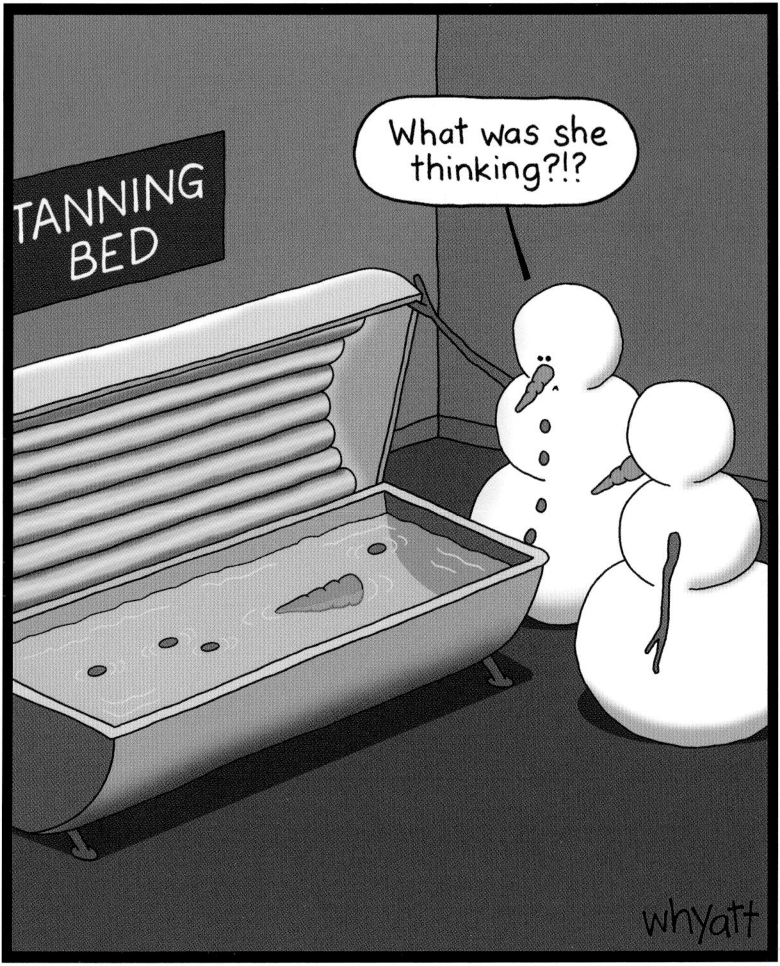
TANNING BED
What was she thinking?!?
whyatt

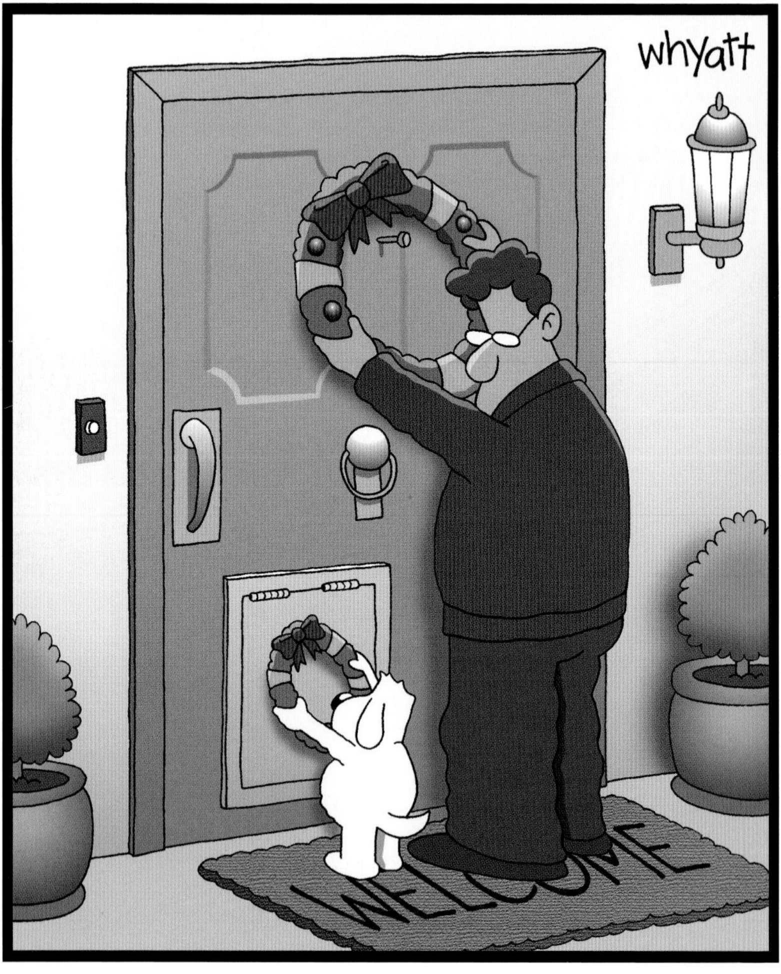
whyatt
WELCOME

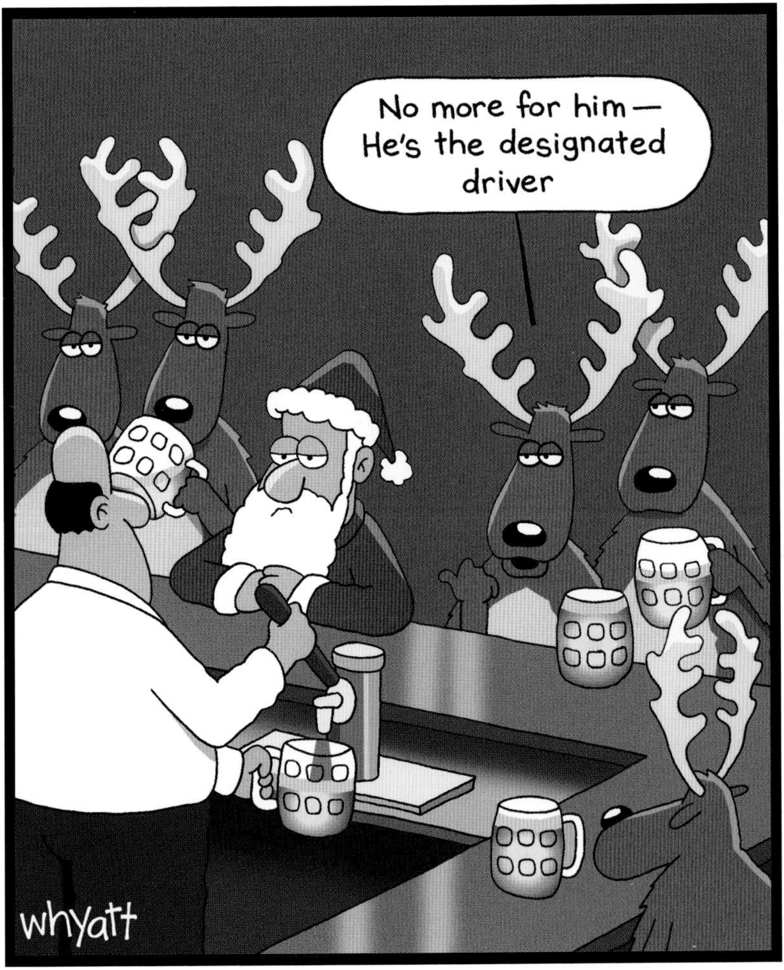
No more for him —
He's the designated
driver
whyatt

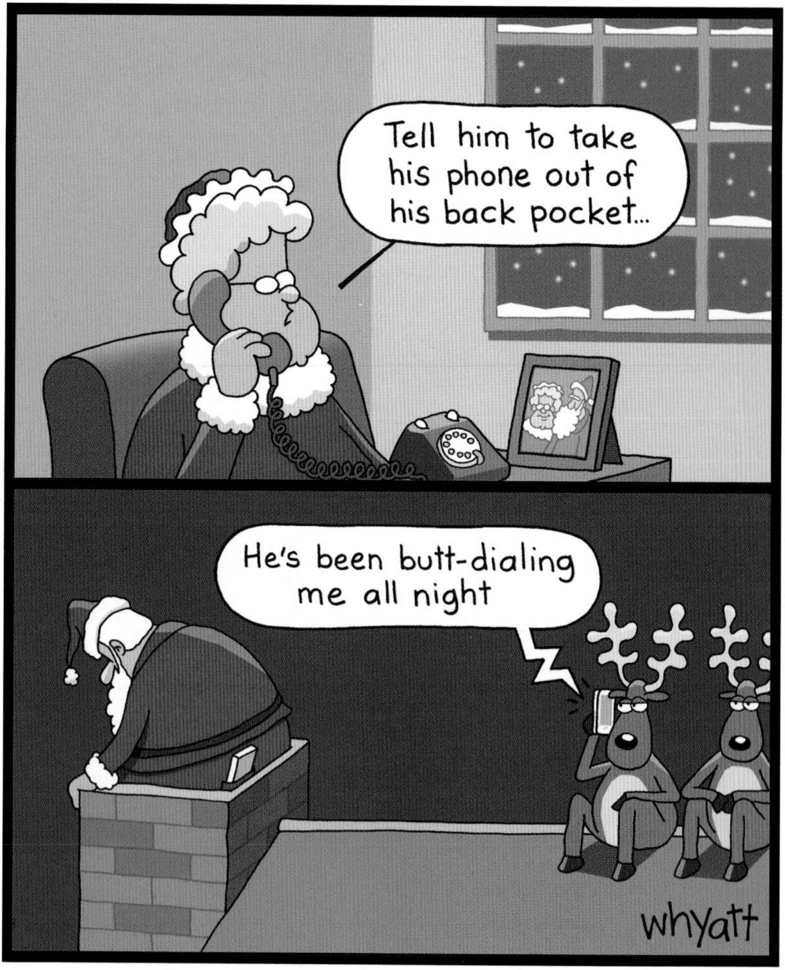
Tell him to take his phone out of his back pocket...
He's been butt-dialing me all night
whyatt

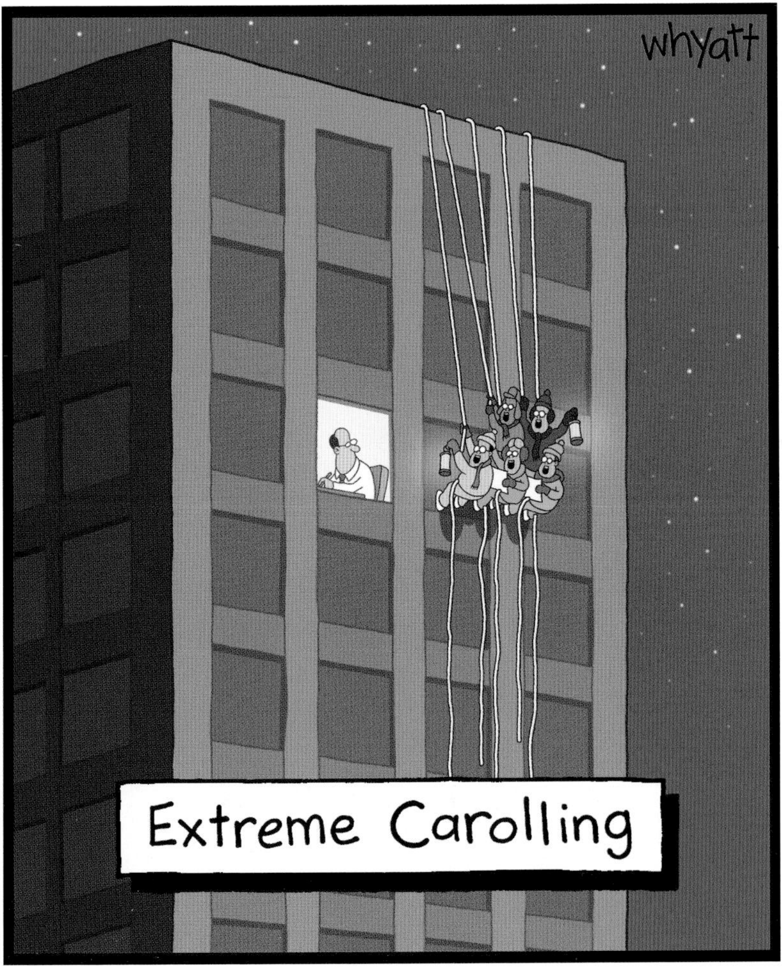
whyatt
Extreme Carolling

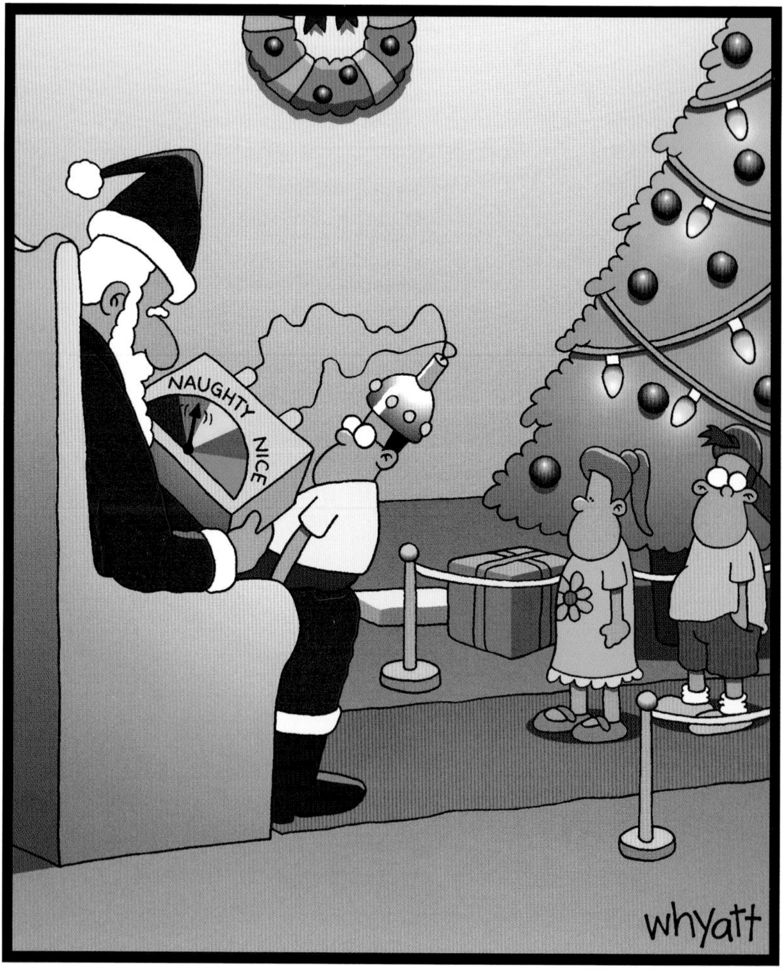
NAUGHTY
NICE
whyatt

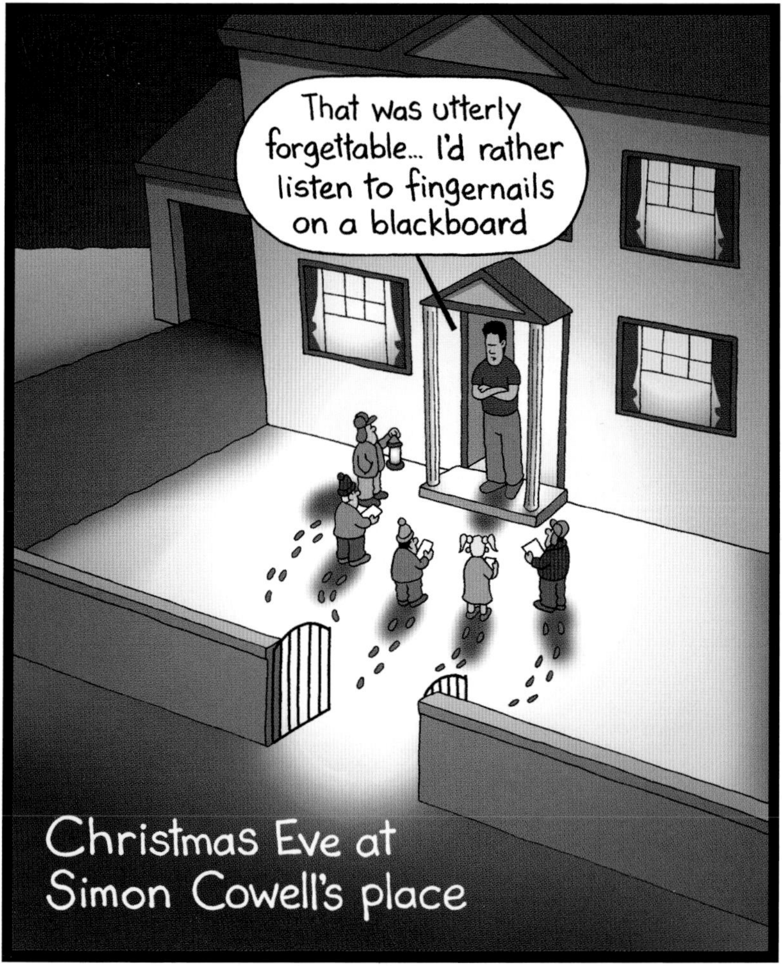
That was utterly forgettable... I'd rather listen to fingernails on a blackboard
Christmas Eve at Simon Cowell's place

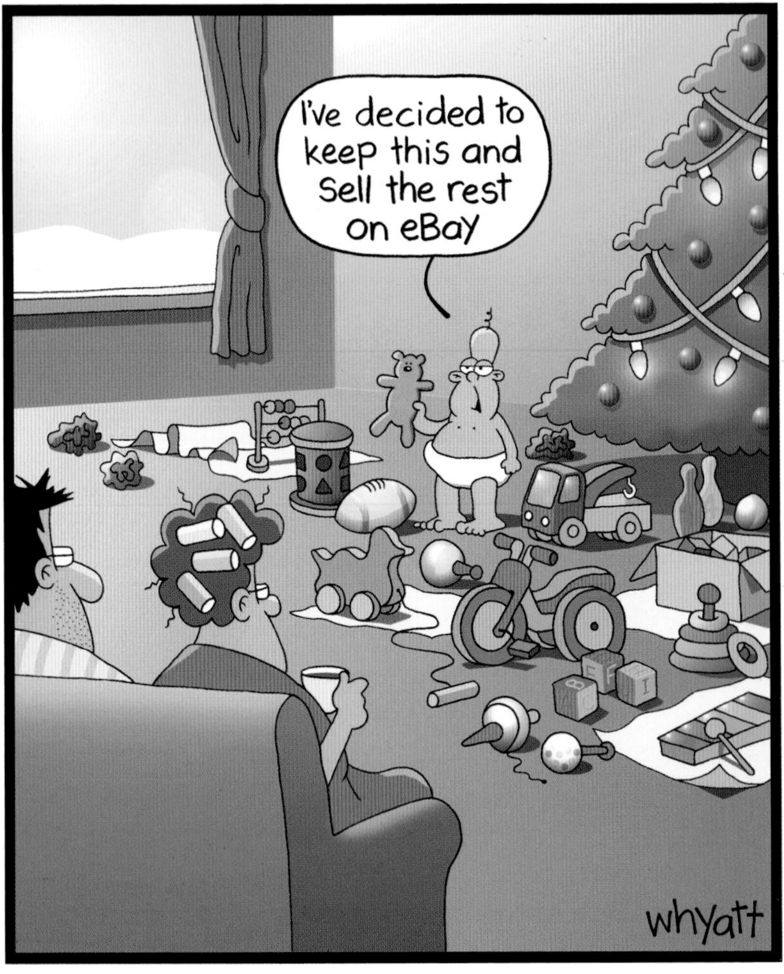
I've decided to keep this and sell the rest on eBay
whyatt

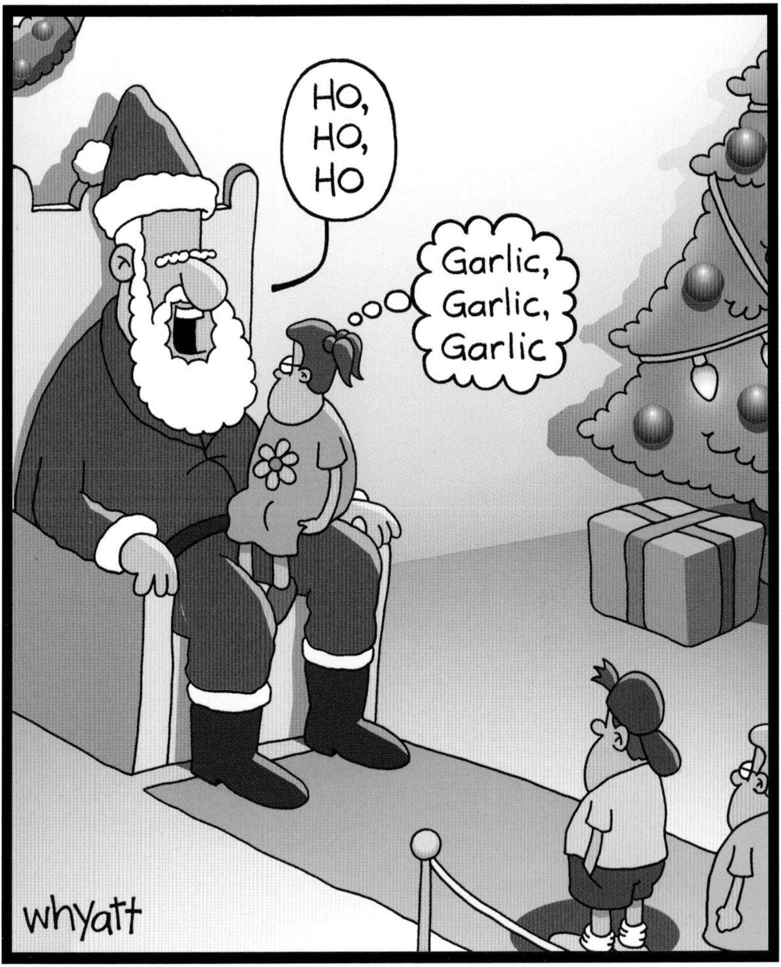
HO, HO, HO
Garlic, Garlic, Garlic
whyatt

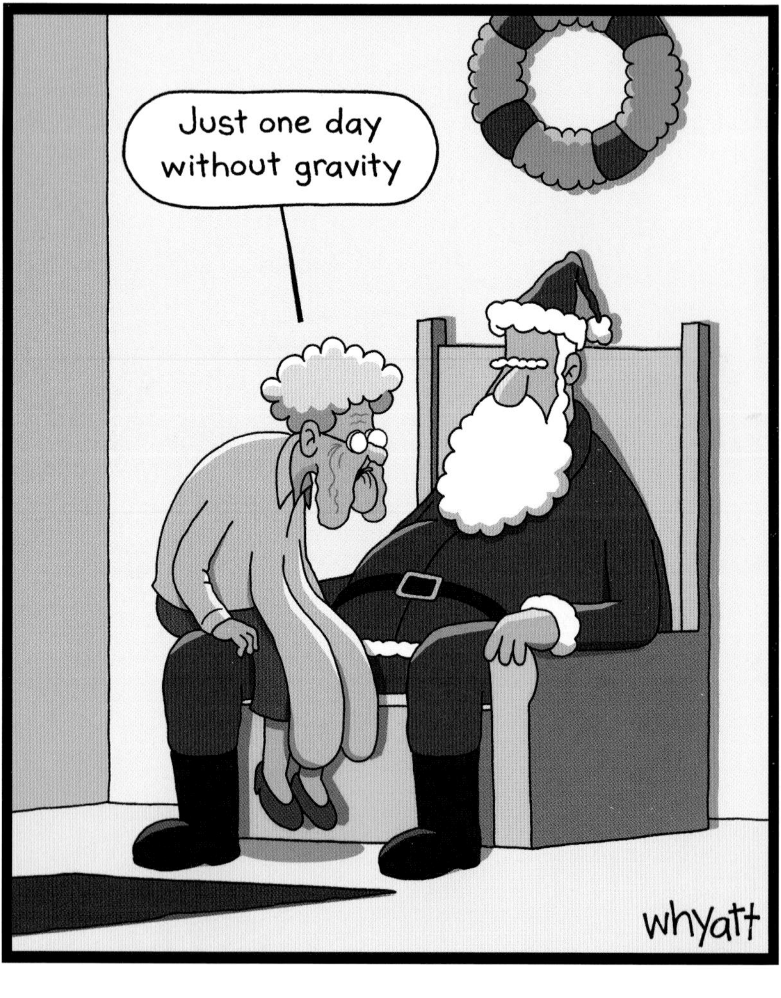
Just one day without gravity
whyatt

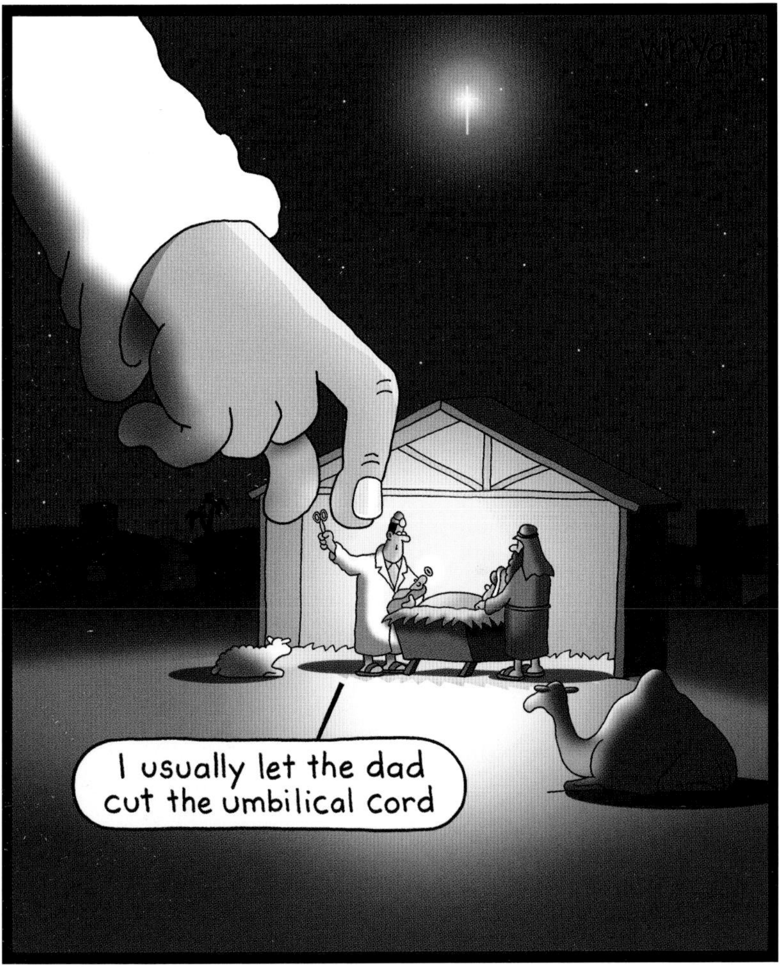
I usually let the dad cut the umbilical cord

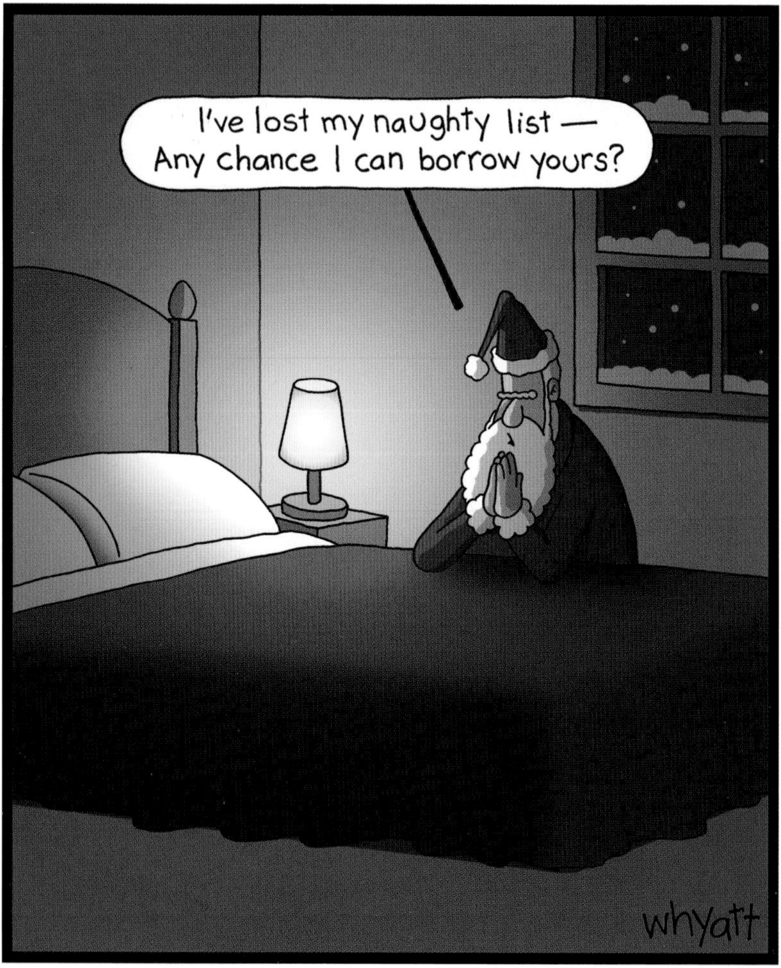
I've lost my naughty list —
Any chance I can borrow yours?
whyatt

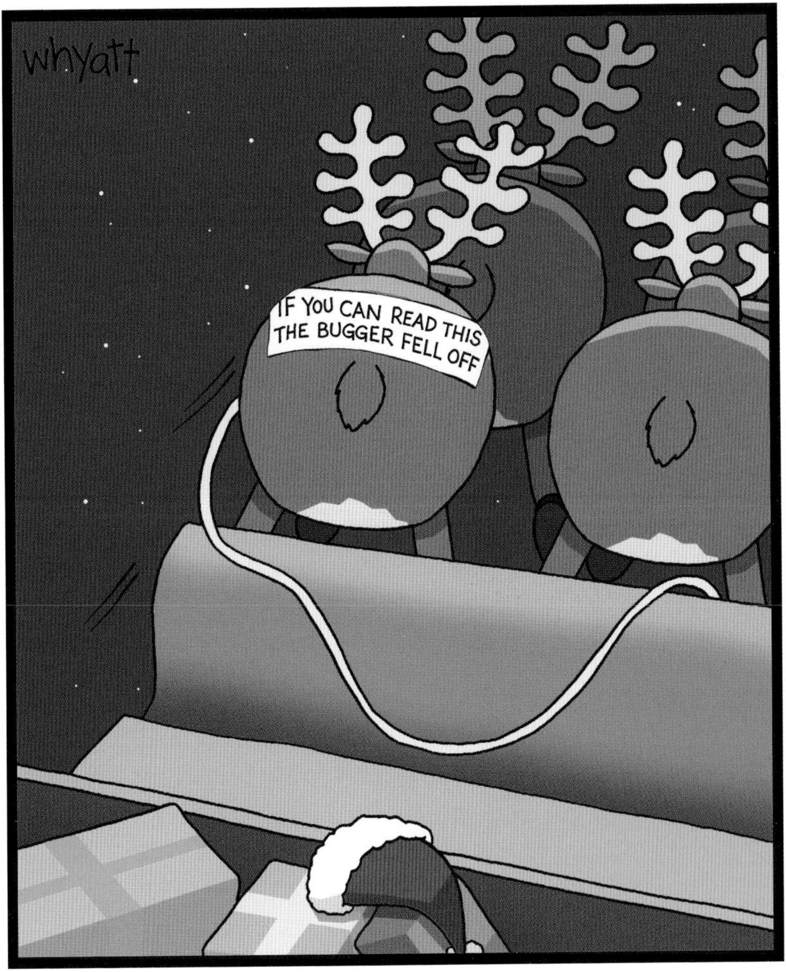
whyatt
IF YOU CAN READ THIS THE BUGGER FELL OFF

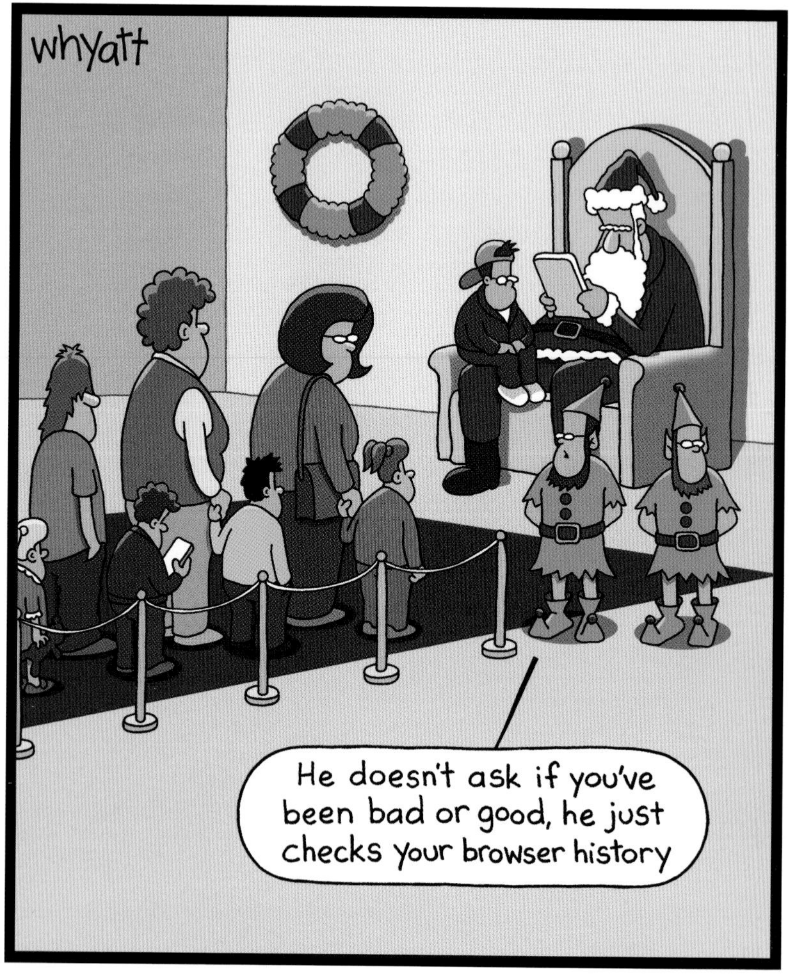
whyatt
He doesn't ask if you've been bad or good, he just checks your browser history

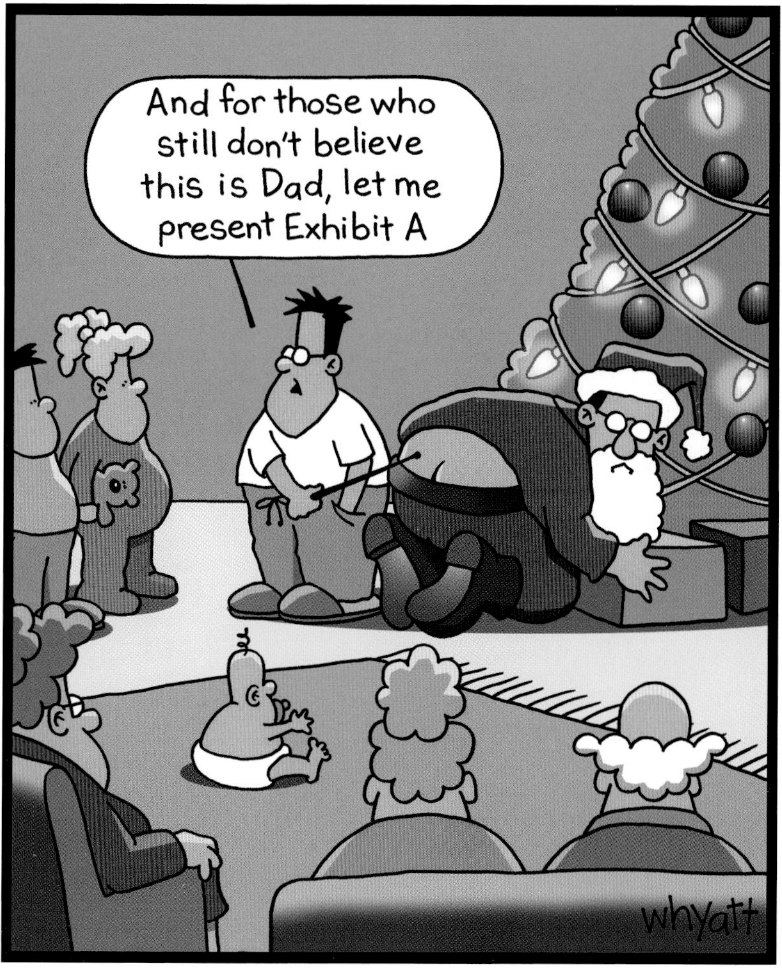
And for those who still don't believe this is Dad, let me present Exhibit A
whyatt

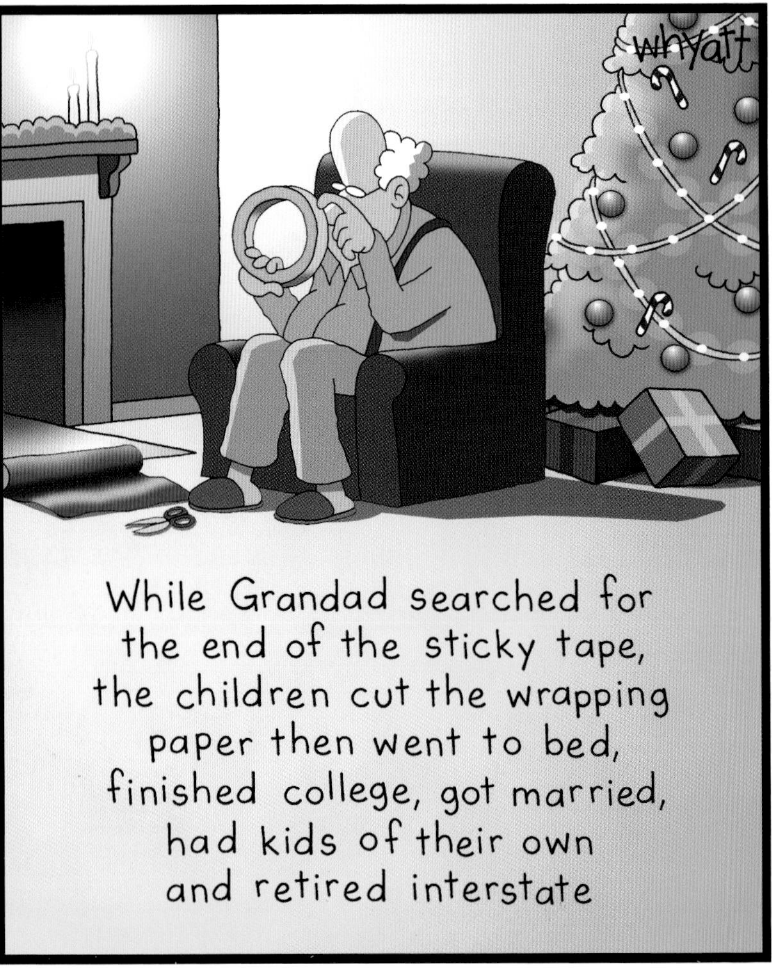
whyatt

While Grandad searched for the end of the sticky tape, the children cut the wrapping paper then went to bed, finished college, got married, had kids of their own and retired interstate

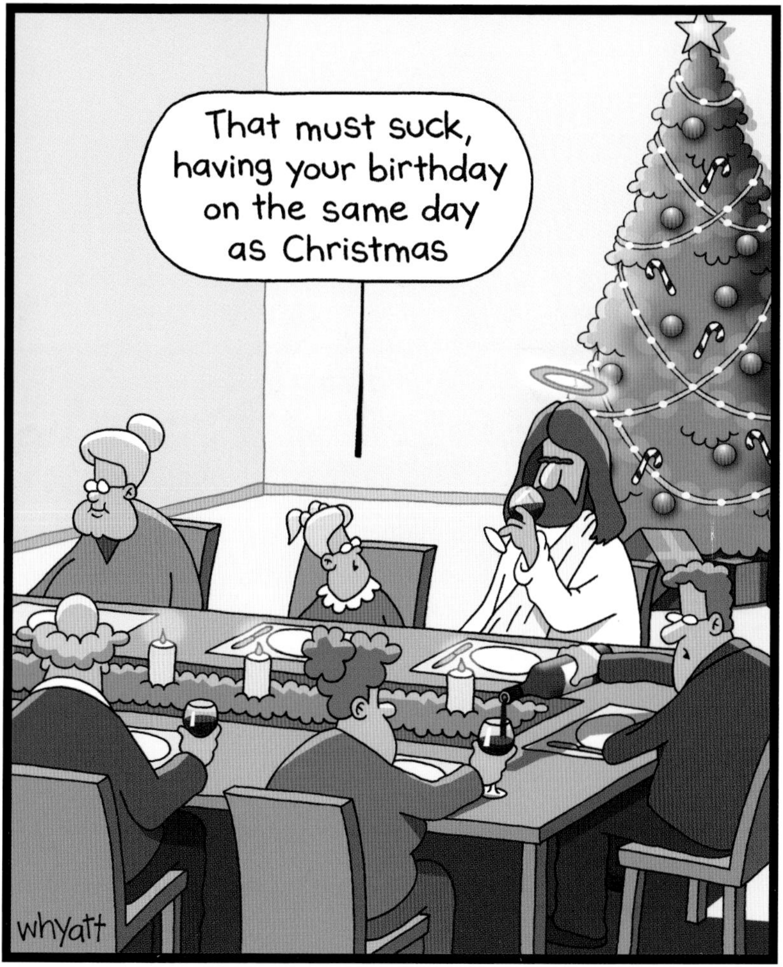
That must suck, having your birthday on the same day as Christmas
whyatt